An Introduction to Economic Inequality

AN INTRODUCTION TO ECONOMIC INEQUALITY

EAMONN BUTLER

Institute of
Economic Affairs

First published in Great Britain in 2022 by
The Institute of Economic Affairs
2 Lord North Street
Westminster
London SW1P 3LB
in association with London Publishing Partnership Ltd
www.londonpublishingpartnership.co.uk

The mission of the Institute of Economic Affairs is to improve understanding of the fundamental institutions of a free society by analysing and expounding the role of markets in solving economic and social problems.

A CIP catalogue record for this book is available from the British Library.

ISBN 978-0-255-36815-5

Many IEA publications are translated into languages other than English or are reprinted. Permission to translate or to reprint should be sought from the Director General at the address above.

Typeset in Kepler by T&T Productions Ltd
www.tandtproductions.com

Printed and bound by Page Bros

CONTENTS

About the author   viii
Acknowledgements   ix
Summary   x
List of figures   xii

1 The inequality debate   1

The consensus on inequality   1
The inequality narrative   2
Questioning the narrative   4

2 Definitions, measures, explanations   7

Meaning and implications   7
Economic inequality   9
Theoretical explanations   10
Measuring income inequality   11

3 Questioning the measurement of incomes   16

Data shortcomings   16
Statistical errors and omissions   18
Who are we comparing?   19
An unreliable picture   20

4 Questioning the measure of wealth   23

Data shortcomings   23

Other confounding factors 26
Who are we comparing? 26
A distortion of the truth 27

5 International comparisons 28

The global inequality narrative 28
Other explanations 30
Equality, poverty and growth 32

6 Must the rich get richer? 35

Wealth is precarious 35
Other forms of wealth 37
Prosperity without equality 37

7 Questioning the moral case 39

The universal humanity argument 39
John Rawls: equality and fairness 41

8 Questioning the practical claims 44

Errors of *The Spirit Level* 44
Misdirecting our focus 48

9 Equal pay in the workplace 49

The contradictions of equal pay 49
Is there a gender pay gap? 51
Are CEOs worth their money? 54

10 The roots of equalisation policy 57

From ethics to politics 57
The impossibility of equal outcomes 58
Compensating bad luck 60

11 Political approaches to equalisation 63

From equality to equity 63

Addressing people's needs   64
Narrowing the differences   66

12 Equality of opportunity   67

The meaning of equal opportunity   68
Should we worry about inheritance?   70

13 Redistribution policies   73

Progressive taxation   73
Wealth taxes   75
Minimum wages   78
Different standards for different groups   79
Economic growth   80

14 Democracy and equality   83

Coalition politics   83
Limits to redistribution   85
Who will equalise the equalisers?   89

15 Barriers to equality   90

Legal and civil equality   90
Equality and mobility   91
Barriers against mobility   92

16 The role of inequality   94

Do people want equality?   94
Equal and unequal societies   95
Wealth and status   96
Growing the pie   98

17 Conclusion   100

References   104

About the IEA   110

ABOUT THE AUTHOR

Eamonn Butler is Director of the Adam Smith Institute, one of the world's leading policy think tanks. He holds degrees in economics and psychology, a PhD in philosophy and an honorary DLitt. In the 1970s he worked in Washington for the US House of Representatives, and taught philosophy at Hillsdale College, Michigan, before returning to the UK to co-found the Adam Smith Institute. He has won the Freedom Medal of Freedoms Foundation at Valley Forge and the UK National Free Enterprise Award; his film *Secrets of the Magna Carta* won an award at the Anthem Film Festival; and his book *Foundations of a Free Society* won the Fisher Prize.

Eamonn's other books include introductions to the pioneering economists Adam Smith, Milton Friedman, F. A. Hayek and Ludwig von Mises. He has also published primers on classical liberalism, public choice, capitalism, democracy, trade, the Austrian School of Economics and great liberal thinkers, as well as *The Condensed Wealth of Nations* and *The Best Book on the Market*. He is co-author of *Forty Centuries of Wage and Price Controls*, and of a series of books on IQ. He is a frequent contributor to print, broadcast and online media.

ACKNOWLEDGEMENTS

Thanks go to many friends for their suggestions and help with sources, and in particular Fiona Townsley of the Adam Smith Institute for her work in researching facts and references.

SUMMARY

The issue of economic inequality has come to dominate the economic and political debate, with mounting numbers of books and articles. Equality is commonly considered as not just good in itself, but something that delivers other values such as health and trust.

At first sight, the statistics look shocking, with a rich few earning most of the world's income and owning most of the world's physical and financial wealth. Inequality has been linked to lower life expectancy, poor education, mental illness, obesity, political instability and other social problems. Campaigners call for taxes on wealth, an expansion of the welfare state and higher minimum wages.

However, there are deep flaws in this narrative.

For example, inequality is hard to measure. While pre-tax incomes look very unequal, taxes and welfare benefits (including access to education, housing and healthcare) reduce the real inequalities in living standards dramatically. Much of the benefit that people get from their work is not just financial, but stimulation, enjoyment and satisfaction.

The inequality statistics are misleading in other ways. People's earnings usually rise over their lifetime, and higher earners can build up more life savings. By bundling older and younger people together, the statistics suggest a wide inequality — and would do, even if every person earned exactly the same amount over their lifetimes.

The policies built on the inequality narrative are also problematic.

Though we talk of the 'income distribution', nobody in fact *distributes* incomes in a conscious way. Incomes are just the outcome of everyone's economic actions. Nor is the pattern of wealth and incomes zero-sum. The fact that someone gets richer does not mean that others must become poorer. Rather, the spread of markets and trade over the last two centuries has made the whole world richer.

Redistribution in the name of equality is contradictory because it requires us to treat people *unequally*. And it ignores the fact that people's economic position reflects their own choices. Some may choose more family time, or job satisfaction, or ease and leisure, over better-paid work.

Critics of the redistribution agenda say that policies such as higher taxes, minimum wages and a bigger welfare state would depress incentives, discouraging work, saving, enterprise and progress. Because politicians would be managing the programme, support would not go to the poor but to groups with greater political influence.

Opinion polls suggest that people dislike *unfairness* but rank other objectives much higher than *equality*. Focusing on inequality may distract us from the real problem: how to create the conditions that will boost the prosperity of everyone.

FIGURES

Figure 1   The Lorenz curve   12

Figure 2   World population living in extreme poverty,
           1820 to 2015   33

1 THE INEQUALITY DEBATE

The consensus on inequality

Economic inequality has become central to much of the academic and political debate, with a rising crescendo of books from economists, academics and social researchers.

Among many, there was economist J. K. Galbraith's denunciation of the excesses of *The Affluent Society* (1958); philosopher John Rawls's claim in *A Theory of Justice* (1971) that inequality is both unfair and irrational; *The Spirit Level* by researchers Kate Pickett and Richard Wilkinson (2010), suggesting that inequality is associated with most social problems; Nobel economist Joseph Stiglitz's view in *The Price of Inequality* (2013) that inequality frays society; and Thomas Piketty's argument in *Capital* (2017) that the rich will always get richer unless faced with a worldwide wealth tax. Politicians have taken up the campaign, with minimum wage policies, increased welfare spending, marginal income tax rates that sometimes approach 100 per cent, and proposals to tax wealth.

So, it seems that there is a consensus on the evils of inequality. Yet, less well heard, there are also plenty of economists, philosophers and social researchers who question the arguments and believe the price of the policies built on them is too high.

The inequality narrative

Shocking statistics. At first sight, the statistics on income inequality look shocking. In Europe, the total income of the top 10 per cent of earners is 10 times that earned by the bottom 50 per cent. In East Asia, Russia and North America, the figure is over 15 times more; in Latin America, South and Southeast Asia, it is over 20 times more; and in Africa and the Middle East, the top 10 per cent earn over 30 times more than the bottom 50 per cent.

The statistics on *wealth* inequality are even more stark. In Europe, the richest 10 per cent appear to own over 60 per cent of total wealth. In North America, South and Southeast Asia it is almost 70 per cent; in Russia, Central Asia, the Middle East, Africa and Latin America it is over 70 per cent. In sum, the world's richest 10 per cent apparently own 76 per cent of the world's wealth and (according to the UN) the richest 1 per cent own 40 per cent of it. Oxfam claims that around two thousand dollar billionaires own more than do 5 billion of the world's poorest.

And the rich seem to be getting richer. In developed countries, the share of income earned by the top 1 per cent fell greatly between the 1920s and 1970s. But over the subsequent five decades, it rose again: the 10 per cent richest Americans quintupled their wealth, while the richest 1 per cent increased theirs sevenfold. Globally, the World Inequality Report indicates that while average wealth has grown at around 3 per cent since 1995, the wealth of the world's richest has grown two or three times that rate. The richest 1 per cent captured nearly two-fifths of all wealth increases since then, while the world's poorest 50 per cent got only two-hundredths of it.

Concerns about inequality. Understandably, this is widely seen as unfair. And self-reinforcing too: inheritance and upbringing give the children of the rich a privileged start in life, and those with money can more easily make money and preserve their privilege. Some inequality critics claim that the rich use their wealth deliberately to keep themselves rich and others poor, pouring money into political parties to secure the election of cronies who will slash taxes for them while curbing welfare spending for others. Poorer families in industrial societies have seen their jobs outsourced to other countries; but the rich have money to spare, and watch their financial investments soar, without any fair taxation to stop it.

The authors of *The Spirit Level* go further, claiming that inequality is linked to lower life expectancy, poorer education, less trust, more mental illness, suicide, obesity, murder and political instability. With more equality, says the UK's Equality Trust, 'murder rates could halve, mental illness could reduce by two thirds, obesity could halve, imprisonment could reduce by 80%, teen births could reduce by 80%, levels of trust could increase by 85%'.

The call for redistribution. Equality is considered self-evidently good: not only fair and just – good in itself – but something that delivers other values such as health, peace and trust. It is also seen as deriving from basic human values – that people are born equal and should enjoy equal opportunities and an equal share of what they all produce. The burden of proof, it is said, is on those who oppose it: before they abandon this obvious good, they must show what benefits they expect to follow.

Meanwhile, the presumption is that we should aim to increase equality. Philanthropy is not enough: only a social and tax revolution will suffice, with progressive income taxes, taxes on wealth, a larger welfare state, more equal provision of basic goods such as health, housing and education, minimum wages, stronger trade unions, anti-discrimination laws and measures to expand employment opportunities.

Or an even bigger revolution. Some campaigners argue that the problem of inequality is intrinsic to capitalism itself and that only a totally different economic system can end it.

Questioning the narrative

This inequality narrative is now so familiar and so widely taken for granted that it is hardly necessary to outline it further. Instead, this book will seek to put the narrative into perspective, and test its claims, by focusing on the criticisms that have been made of it – criticisms that are significant and widespread, but that struggle to receive the same attention.

Measurement problems. For example, critics of the narrative point out that income inequality is hard to measure. Money isn't everything: people also get a 'psychological income' from jobs that are satisfying, stimulating and pleasant; but that cannot be measured. Moreover, while pre-tax incomes look very unequal, they are much less so after tax. And state benefits, such as welfare and pensions, go mainly to the poor. What we all ultimately get to *consume* is much more equal.

Then there is the problem that people's earnings usually rise over their lifetimes (and wealth more so, as older people on higher incomes can save more), so the statistics exaggerate inequality by comparing people at different life stages.

Much wealth, such as that held by governments or companies, does not even enter the calculations, leaving us with the false impression that most wealth is controlled by a few rich individuals. Moreover, wealth fluctuates, as the prices of people's assets (such as stocks, bonds, property or cars) go up or down. Indeed, if there is a financial crash and everyone's wealth shrinks, but the assets of the rich shrink even more, equality would increase, even though everyone is worse off: is that what we want?

Unequal treatment. 'Equality' and 'income distribution', say these critics, are loaded terms: we are really talking about *differences* in outcomes. Those just happen, for good reasons and bad, but nobody consciously 'distributes' them. *Redistribution* in the name of that equality is a contradiction because it requires us to treat people unequally – taking from some, giving to others. Moreover, people differ in countless non-financial ways – such as family background or natural abilities like strength or attractiveness – all of which may affect their earning capacity but are impossible to measure. And people's fortunes also depend on their own choices: to compensate people for bad choices may simply encourage more bad choices.

Policy problems. The policies being proposed to reduce inequality, such as progressive taxes and higher state benefits, would depress incentives, say the critics, discouraging work, saving, enterprise, innovation, progress and prosperity. Their revenues would not go to the poor but would be distributed according to groups' political strength. In any case, state programmes are not exactly fair – the provision of schooling, for example, is hardly 'equal' if you have no children to benefit from it. And the politicians and officials in charge of all this redistribution would need vast powers, which could be abused.

Other concerns. Polls suggest that people object to *unfairness*, but rate other issues higher than *inequality*. Most simply want to work hard and get ahead, not live in an equal society. Indeed, people risk their lives to migrate to other countries in pursuit of freedom and fortune, not equality.

Rather than strive to produce an impossible *equality* of wealth, say the critics, we should focus on *creating* wealth. They advocate equal legal and political rights, but otherwise removing barriers against people's self-improvement and treating them as free and diverse individuals. This may produce big differences in income and wealth, but if it makes *everyone* better off and ends poverty, what humane person would not prefer it?

2 DEFINITIONS, MEASURES, EXPLANATIONS

Meaning and implications

The popular narrative suggests that more equality in wealth and incomes is self-evidently good, that only the wealthy would dispute this, that government action is needed to make the change, and that, since equality affects everything, it must take precedence over other political objectives. The reality is not so straightforward.

Few people think through the meaning and implications of the inequality narrative. For a start, as mentioned, human beings are naturally unequal in many ways. Their age, strength, abilities, talent and personality may all affect their earning potential – though we cannot say by how much: we simply cannot measure most of these individual characteristics, far less equalise them. That may be why the inequality narrative focuses on income and wealth, which *are* potentially measurable and manipulable. But even if we could equalise people's wealth and incomes, they would still remain unequal in many other ways.

And would equalisation be a fair and just thing to do anyway? If some people earn more and acquire more wealth because they are extremely diligent, industrious and thrifty, while others earn and acquire less because they are not, should we ignore those moral differences and try to leave them economically equal anyway? To do so would hardly encourage responsibility and prudence.

Loaded terms. The debate is not helped by *inequality* and *equality* being loaded terms. The words do not only mean difference and similarity; they also suggest that similarity is good and difference is bad. That prompts people to go beyond merely *understanding* human differences and to set about *changing* them – which may or may not be a wise thing to do.

The phrases *distribution of income* and *distribution of wealth* are also misleading. As a statistical term, *distribution* means only the incidence of some feature, such as how many people there are in each age group. But in everyday use, *distribution* suggests that income or wealth are not *earned*, but that some person or body – such as 'society' – is purposefully *allocating* them.

The confusion is magnified when we then talk about the *share* of income enjoyed by different groups, as if income is a pie being divided between a family. Again, the term *share* – and talk of people's *fair share* – suggests that *equal* shares are the only moral outcome.

Hence, the language of the equality debate pushes us into believing that we can and *should* alter income and wealth differences. The discussion might proceed more clearly if we jettisoned these terms and talked only about economic *differences* and the *spread* of incomes and wealth. Unfortunately, the debate is too far gone for this. But when we use terms such as *inequality* and *distribution*, we should remember that they are descriptions, not prescriptions.

Economic inequality

Economic inequality, the main subject of this book, is about differences in wealth or income. *Income* is the flow of benefits (usually money) that someone earns from a job or business or as rent on property or dividends from investments. (Rent or dividends are sometimes differentiated as *unearned income* – another loaded term, which forgets that property and assets must generally be worked and saved for, and so are indeed *earned*.)

Wealth is the value of the stock of assets that someone acquires, such as land, housing or cars, plus financial assets such as stocks and bonds. There are feedbacks between income and wealth: the more income someone has, the more property they can acquire; and the more property they have, the more income they can derive from it.

But *inequality* is not the same as *poverty*. Populations can be equal but poor or unequal but rich. For instance, the US is less equal than many other countries but it is richer than most. Myanmar is more equal than most others but is poorer than most others too. Two subsistence farmers in Burundi may be equal, but they are equal in their poverty.

Again, we need to use the term *poverty* with care. It may mean *absolute* poverty, the specific level of deprivation experienced by some person or group. (Though even here, our notion of deprivation changes over time – things considered essential today, such as hot running water, were thought luxuries a century ago.) But it may also refer to *relative poverty*, where people earn less than the national average – usually defined as less than 60 per cent of the median income. Once more, we must use caution: people in a rich country who are below the relative poverty line may still be very well off, while people in a poor country who are above the relative poverty line may not be well off at all.

Remember too, that even if some economic boom doubled everyone's income, the numbers in *relative* poverty would remain the same.

Equality is also not the same as *equity*. Economic equality means identical wealth or income – an objective measure. Equity is the distribution of incomes or wealth that is considered acceptable. And that is subjective.

Theoretical explanations

There are many theoretical explanations for economic inequality. Karl Marx saw it as the historic result of economic power and the exploitation of workers. The sociologist Max Weber thought that differences in social status, ownership and political power created hierarchies that were then reflected in incomes. Modern feminists might attribute it to patriarchy and the glass ceiling. Neoliberals see it as merely the objective outcome of impersonal market processes – and argue that it would be lower, were it not for government interventions that create concentrations of economic and political power. But there is no shortage of other explanations.

In practical terms, market conditions have effects on inequality. Globalisation, for example, has prompted producers in industrial countries to outsource manufacturing jobs to cheaper countries, and has increased the demand for high-skill workers in finance and IT – widening the existing income differences.

Governments may unwittingly increase inequality too. Regressive taxes on essentials such as housing or fuel or clothing disadvantage poorer people, for whom these are a greater part of the household budget. Welfare provision may see more people sticking on relatively low social benefits rather than seeking work. And so on.

Social changes can also make a difference. For example, a large influx of immigrants with low education or skill levels may put a further downward pressure on already low wages. So too might the increase in the numbers of women in work, many of them opting for (less well-paid) flexible or part-time work. The rise in single-person or single-parent households and in two-earner households also widens household income differences. And an ageing population may mean that there are more people who no longer earn, but who have more saved wealth.

Measuring income inequality

The standard way of measuring income inequality starts with the Lorenz curve, developed by the US economist Max Lorenz. On the horizontal axis is the cumulative number of earners, from poorest to richest, while on the vertical is the cumulative percentage of total income they received. If there were complete equality, with each *x* percentile of the population receiving the same *x* percentile of income, this would produce a straight 45° line on the graph. The more inequality there is, the more the curve bulges out below the 45° line.

Figure 1   The Lorenz curve

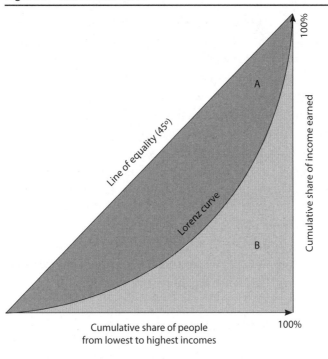

Line of equality (45°)

Lorenz curve

A

B

100%

Cumulative share of income earned

Cumulative share of people
from lowest to highest incomes

100%

From this is derived the Gini coefficient, named after the Italian statistician Corrado Gini – the ratio of the area between the curve and the 45° line (A) to the total area below the 45° line (B). The higher the ratio, the more the inequality. A Gini coefficient of 0 would mean complete equality; a coefficient of 1 would mean complete inequality, with all the income going to a single person.

This calculation throws up some interesting results. The annual calculations by World Population Review show that many African countries (e.g. South Africa, Namibia) show up as highly unequal, with several Latin American countries (e.g. Colombia, Venezuela) not far behind. Many former Soviet states (e.g. Ukraine, Slovenia) appear as much more equal, with Nordic countries (e.g. Finland, Iceland) coming close behind. The US, though commonly branded as highly unequal, only just makes it into the most unequal third of countries, while the UK appears in the most equal third.

Shortcomings. Unfortunately, the Gini coefficient is very sensitive to 'outliers', meaning that a few very wealthy individuals can change the number greatly, even in a large population. Other measures are less sensitive to this problem, such as the Palma ratio (the proportion of gross national income earned by the highest-earning 10 per cent divided by that of the lowest-earning 40 per cent) and the Kuznets ratio (the same for the highest 20 per cent and lowest 40 per cent). Yet these measures still tell us nothing about the exact *nature* of the inequalities within a country (such as differences between different ethnic, age or gender groups), nor why they come about.

Trends. While the Gini coefficient is a crude and potentially very misleading measure, it remains the one most usually cited in the inequality debate. And it might at least reveal trends: for example, it suggests that between the 1920s and 1980s, inequality in the developed countries fell – something commonly attributed to more universal access to welfare support and education. Then, since 1990, inequality within some developed countries such as the US seems to have risen – commonly attributed to globalisation, economic growth, tax reductions that help the well-off, immigration and weaker trade unions that leave poorer workers less able to demand and get pay rises. But in other places, such as the EU and UK, the trend is much less pronounced.

Both the upward and downward trends of recent decades are almost certainly a result of many causes. But it is hard to measure the impact of any one of them. Globalisation may be a strong factor, since it has raised the demand for (already well-paid) top talent and has seen (less well-paid) manufacturing jobs being outsourced to developing countries. Recent tax reductions may well leave the well-off even better off, but a more powerful effect might be that they induce former tax exiles to return home and attract in wealthier people from other countries.

For the most part, though, migrants tend to be poorer, so the rising number of migrants – now 12 per cent of developed countries' populations, up from 7 per cent in 1990, according to the International Monetary Fund – would have increased inequality. Trade unions have become weaker since state monopoly industries in several countries were privatised. But the modern economy rests much more on smaller, competitive firms so that although pay bargaining is more local, that does not mean it is any weaker. And again, spurts in economic growth are commonly associated with rising inequality, but growth has been much stronger in the developing countries than the richer industrial ones, so it may not be a strong factor in the rising inequality there.

Benign inequality? Looking through these possible factors, it is important to realise that some causes of inequality may be undesirable, while others may be benign. Growth and globalisation, for example, have positive effects on general prosperity, regardless of their impact on Gini coefficients. Weaker trade unions may be due more to economic change and progress than to any political campaign to weaken them. Lower taxes may help a country to get back its flight capital and attract new investment that will help it to prosper in future years. Inequality, in other words, may be a result of positive changes that also benefit the poorest.

3 QUESTIONING THE MEASUREMENT OF INCOMES

Data shortcomings

As well as being limited in what it tells us, the Gini coefficient also relies on limited and questionable information. Different countries measure income data in different ways, and with different degrees of accuracy, making international comparisons unreliable. International agencies such as the World Bank and the International Monetary Fund try to compensate for these differences, but there is no perfect way of doing so.

Even within countries, income information is incomplete. For instance, the US Current Population Survey of household incomes captures only money receipts, not capital gains, and top incomes are not reported for reasons of confidentiality. The US Treasury Statistics of Income is more complete for top earners but less so for lower earners, and does not capture age, educational qualifications and other factors that might help us understand the extent and nature of income inequalities.

Trend data are also confused by the annual changes in tax codes that alter what is reported as income, plus the volatility of business profits and losses. And the Gini approach does not deal well with in-kind state benefits such as Medicare in the US and the NHS in the UK, which greatly equalise what goods and services people access.

Taxes and benefits. Gini results depend greatly on whether income is assessed before or after tax. In the UK, for example, the top 1 per cent of earners pay well over a third of all income tax receipts, according to the Institute for Fiscal Studies. The top 20 per cent of UK earners have twelve times the income of the bottom 20 per cent; but after tax and state benefits are included, that comes down to just four times, according to the Office for National Statistics (2021). Likewise the Congressional Budget Office (2021) reports that means-tested benefits increased the income of the lowest fifth of US earners by 68 per cent, while taxes reduced the income of the top fifth by 24 per cent.

Furthermore, in-kind public benefits such as universal education, healthcare and subsidised transport are distributed very equally, as is the provision of local facilities such as parks, policing, sports facilities, care of the elderly, roads and refuse collection; but they are not included in the statistics.

In other words, there is already an equalisation system, which is working as intended. Economists generally quote Gini coefficients based on post-tax and post-benefit 'disposable' incomes. But we must be wary of campaigners using the raw income data, before tax and benefits are included, which greatly exaggerate real inequality in terms of people's actual standard of living.

Statistical errors and omissions

Even the strictly *financial* statistics are questionable. For a start, there are too few earners at the very top to provide reliable information, and many of those have irregular income, sometimes making large profits and sometimes large losses.

Shadow economy. Another factor overlooked in the statistics is undeclared income – the shadow or 'back pocket' economy. The higher marginal tax rates are, the larger this is likely to be. According to a 2018 IMF working paper, the UK's shadow economy is over 6 per cent of Gross Domestic Product – and that is low by European standards. In Spain it is over 11 per cent, in Greece over 14 per cent, and in Bulgaria an astonishing 19 per cent.

Untaxed 'back pocket' income probably benefits lower-income people most, and its omission from the official figures inflates the inequality figures. It is true that many top earners manipulate tax rules to minimise their reported income, which might make reported incomes look more equal; but the much more widespread shadow economy almost certainly swamps this effect.

Living standards. Though taxes, social and in-kind benefits and undeclared income are not counted in the statistics, they greatly equalise the standard of living that everyone can afford. Meanwhile, today's near-universal access to important goods and services such as the Internet, television, phones and kitchen appliances is another great but unmeasured equaliser. So are workplace 'fringe' benefits, such as employer-paid health insurance (hugely important in the US) or pensions (particularly important in the Netherlands, Iceland, Switzerland, Australia and the UK), which again make real inequality far less than it appears.

Who are we comparing?

Most income statistics focus on *household* incomes. Using *individual* incomes makes inequality look far greater. A household with one high earner, a non-employed partner and two student children, for example, will look very unequal in terms of income, even though all four share the same standard of living. By contrast, a similar household in which all four hold jobs will suggest that there is no income inequality at all.

But households are so diverse that comparing them is not easy. The rise in the number of non-earning students and carers, for example, may explain some of the apparent rise in equality, even though these non-earners are not necessarily living poorly. Likewise, the rise in both single-person households and multiple-earner households tends to inflate the inequality figures.

Other social factors. Other social factors affect the measures too. The migration of poorer people into richer countries has already been mentioned. And in a few places, such as London and New York, inflows of super-rich migrants widen the apparent inequality even more. But these may be merely temporary surges, rather than causes of long-term inequality.

However, the most significant factor is *age*. People's incomes tend to grow over their lifetimes. Typically, they start on low wages – or if they are in education or training for a profession, they might earn nothing at all. Then as they acquire more experience, skills, contacts, status and confidence, their income rises. Then it falls off again as they retire and live on savings. Even if each person earned *precisely the same total income over their lifetimes*, the statistics would still show marked inequalities because the statistics take a panoramic snapshot of everyone, including both the low-income young and the high-income old.

Unproblematic inequality. To the extent that Gini measures conceal factors such as this large age effect, perhaps we should not worry about them too much. After all, the top 20 per cent earners of today may be the same people who were at the bottom 20 per cent 40 years ago; and today's poor migrants may be tomorrow's millionaire entrepreneurs. Rather, we should remember that inequality statistics may reflect phenomena that most people would regard as unproblematic. High inequality measures do not necessarily indicate that something bad is going on.

An unreliable picture

Factors such as the composition of households, the nature of the workforce, the age of the population, the value of state benefits, and how we measure inflation, therefore, are all critical to the Gini coefficient. Adjusting for such factors can create the *opposite* picture to the one of large and widening inequality that dominates the public debate.

Ignoring the unmeasurable. Another problem is that the income statistics measure only money. But much of the benefit we get from work is not financial. Some people might *willingly* take lower wages to work in a more spiritually rewarding job – perhaps with agreeable colleagues, doing safe, clean, non-stressful work in a nice environment. Others might prefer to have more money for doing dirty, disagreeable or dangerous jobs in unpleasant conditions. Some may consciously opt for low-paid but flexible or part-time working to have time for family responsibilities, and others not. Some may give up present earnings to train for a better job, and others not.

Such choices depend on people's personal assessment of the value of their sacrifice. That is not something we can measure, but it has large consequences for the inequality calculations. People's choices may leave them *financially* unequal, but if we could measure the non-financial benefits they enjoy, there is likely to be far less difference.

Consumption. In any case, money incomes are only half the story: the real question is what they buy for people. The inequality narrative suggests that since the late 1970s, the incomes of the highest earners have been rising while those of the lowest earners have 'stagnated', widening inequality.

This is a sweeping generalisation. In recent years, measured inequality has risen in some developed countries (such as the US) but not all. For instance, research for the World Inequality Lab by Marc Morgan and Theresa Neef (2020) suggests that, while inequality in Europe rose from the mid 1980s to the mid 1990s, it has since remained fairly flat; and the post-tax income of the top 10 per cent of earners is narrowing back towards that of the bottom 50 per cent.

Moreover, the 'widening inequality' claim ignores the equalising factors of state benefits and public services. And it also ignores the huge price falls (and quality improvements) in what we buy, made possible by soaring productivity, technology and globalisation. To name but a few: cars, medicines, home appliances and electronic goods have all become vastly cheaper. That has benefited poorer families in particular – there are limits to the number of phones or dishwashers that higher earners can use. Better and cheaper food, healthcare, transport and clothing have boosted the living standards of the poor more than anyone's.

Meanwhile, life expectancy has risen markedly, and infant mortality is now a rarity. People work fewer hours and take longer holidays. This is not 'stagnation', but a marked improvement that benefits lower earners the most. It narrows the real differences in living standards, but the statistics fail to account for it. As an indicator of whether living standards have improved, the Gini, Palma and Kuznets measures of income inequality are far from perfect.

4 QUESTIONING THE MEASURE OF WEALTH

Data shortcomings

Wealth is even more difficult to measure than incomes, for many of the same reasons. There are too few billionaires on which to base reliable statistics. The value of assets, such as houses or company shares, varies from year to year or even day to day, making a person's 'wealth' hard to put a figure on. And while governments monitor incomes for tax purposes, assets are generally taxed only when they are sold, so we have only a fuzzy picture of how many people own how much wealth, and therefore no precise measure of wealth inequality.

Information from estates. The classic way to assess wealth differences is to examine the estates of the dead, which *are* recorded for tax purposes. But this method may provide only a very distorted picture. For example, assets such as cars, jewellery, cash and household goods are often under-valued (or not declared) by families seeking to avoid estate taxes. And since these are very common assets, and form a large part of smaller estates, the effect is to make small estates seem even smaller, widening the apparent inequality.

Also, people who die tend to be older and (given the life-cycle effect) wealthier than the average. So they are not fully representative of what is happening in the general population. And since they are only a small sample of the whole population, statistics based on them are sensitive to outliers; the death of a single billionaire will raise the apparent inequality recorded in any one year.

State entitlements. Another widely held but ignored form of wealth is the value of state benefits and services. State benefits such as welfare and pensions provide their recipients with a cash income that may last over many years. We can put a capital value on that income stream – think of it as the amount of money you would need to put in a savings account to produce an equal stream of interest payments. This guaranteed regular income from the state is therefore a form of wealth. It is not included in the official figures, but it makes a big difference. According to research by Lindsay Jacobs and colleagues (2021) for the Federal Reserve Bank of Boston, the value of pensions and social security in the US amounts to half of all wealth. Adding them produces a markedly lower figure for wealth inequality.

State services, such as schools and hospitals, also provide people with a stream of non-financial benefits. They too are a form of wealth with a capital value: think of it in terms of how much money you would need to invest to afford these continuing services. But again, this form of wealth is not counted. In some countries with highly developed welfare states, the capital value of these state benefits and services may well exceed all other forms of personal wealth. And, being available to everyone, they have a powerful, but unrecorded, equalising effect.

This patchy accounting is particularly misleading when the US statistics, for example, include private pensions but not public pensions, and home ownership but not housing subsidies. These omissions exaggerate inequality but have little justification.

Negative wealth. A further statistical snag is that many people are recorded as having 'negative wealth' though they are not necessarily poor. Even rich people have mortgages and debts. New graduates of American and European medical schools may begin work carrying large student loans, even though many come from wealthy households and can look forward to future earnings well above the average. Including such cases in the crude statistics (as Oxfam, in its annual inequality ratings, used to do, before accepting the criticism) inflates apparent wealth inequalities.

Human capital. The most significant omission from the wealth statistics is perhaps human capital, the economic value that people build up in their own experience and skills. This includes assets such as education, training, skills and good health, which make them more productive and useful to employers. This form of wealth is impossible to measure, but it is something we all have to some extent; it is therefore far more equally spread throughout the population than is physical wealth. Again, its omission makes wealth inequality look wider than it is.

Other confounding factors

A quirk, but an important one, in wealth inequality measures is that, if the assets of wealthier people fall in value (as happened during the financial crash of 2008–9), then measured equality rises – even though nobody is better off, and the investors are much worse off. We must not confuse equality with prosperity.

Taxation is another problem. Different assets are taxed in different ways, affecting their prices, and the taxation of financial assets changes frequently, upsetting the wealth (and therefore equality) statistics. Inflation too distorts the value of different assets, eroding the value of some (such as cash savings) while boosting the demand for others (such as gold or property).

Who are we comparing?

As with income, life cycles can confuse the statistics. Since people's incomes generally rise over their lifetimes, older people can save more than younger people. So their wealth grows, even more significantly than their incomes. Even if there were complete lifetime equality, with each person retiring with *precisely the same total savings*, the statistics will still suggest huge inequality because they are comparing younger, poorer individuals with older, richer ones. And with longevity rising, there are more older and richer people around, further exaggerating the differences.

Because so much personal wealth is held in land and housing, rises in property values have the effect of increasing wealth inequality. In some countries such as the UK, significant rises in house prices have been a major driver of the apparent increase in wealth inequality. Those with property (mostly older people) have seen the value of their property assets rise, those without (mostly younger people) have missed out on that increase.

Indeed, in the UK case, this housing inequality has been *increased* by state action, not alleviated by it. Planning controls that restrict the building of new houses and the conversion of older ones depress the available supply of homes, while immigration and benefits policies, including subsidies for some home-buyers, raise the demand, resulting in soaring property values. Again, we should remember that state intervention is not necessarily the antidote to inequality but is often its cause.

A distortion of the truth

The Gini coefficient is therefore bound to suggest an even greater inequality of wealth than of income; but it remains an unreliable guide to the real situation, and highly sensitive to the quality of the data employed.

Remember too that much wealth is not held by individuals but by governments (controlled by legislatures) and companies (controlled by shareholders). The notion of a few billionaires controlling most of the world's wealth is an exaggeration. And anyway, if people accumulate wealth from working hard, saving prudently and investing wisely, so adding to economic growth and general prosperity, is that not something to applaud rather than condemn?

5 INTERNATIONAL COMPARISONS

The global inequality narrative

The narrative on global inequality is well known: inequality has been growing for decades; billionaires are making trillions while workers' earnings are falling by trillions; the richest 1 per cent own two-fifths of the world's wealth; the top ten billionaires have more wealth between them than do a number of countries; the richest are getting richer while the poorest are falling into debt; the top 1 per cent have captured twice as much of the world's economic growth as the bottom 50 per cent; and these inequalities are reflected in poverty and poor access to healthcare, housing, sanitation, education and opportunity.

Data problems. We should be sceptical of these claims, given the problems of data collection discussed above. It is hard enough to get accurate measures within a single country, let alone make comparisons between countries, when income and wealth data are collected in different ways and with different accuracy. Quirks such as exchange rates also confuse the picture: since general prices in poor countries are low, they can look even poorer. That can be compensated by using purchasing power parity (PPP) instead of raw prices; but it is always wise to check that the figures that are thrown out in the public debate reflect this.

Unreliable explanations. The traditional explanations of global inequality are also both familiar and questionable. Colonialism and slavery are suggested, though colonies imposed costs on the occupying powers as well as delivering them benefits. Slavery, as Adam Smith noted, was not only morally offensive but bad economics too.

Differences in natural resources are also cited, though places such as Hong Kong and Singapore prospered even without this advantage. More important is probably whether such potential wealth is controlled by rulers, cronies or oligarchs – as is the absence of a rule of law, allowing those insiders to plunder.

Famine and natural disasters (such as earthquakes) are also blamed; but where markets are allowed to work, famine has been largely eliminated, while rising standards and international collaboration has greatly reduced loss of life from natural disasters.

Another notion is that since poorer countries generally depend on exporting commodities, for which the demand is limited, they will always lag those producing manufactures, where demand is infinite. But several poorer countries have leapfrogged into advanced technologies, undermining this claim.

A final explanation, globalisation, has certainly seen some poor-country producers undercut by more efficiently made imports. On the other hand, incomes in countries such as Bangladesh, Vietnam and the Philippines are rising enormously as richer countries have outsourced work to them.

Other explanations

There are more convincing explanations.

Cultural factors. Cultural differences, such as the refusal in some places to let women work outside the home, or to allow low-status groups into professions, are obviously significant. Wars and civil wars, often between different religious or ethnic groups, interrupt investment and growth. Sometimes such violence ignites because a country is ruled by force rather than through democratic consent; in other words, civil institutions are crucial too.

Institutional and policy differences. Then there are policy mistakes such as import substitution – the attempt to produce at home things that can be bought more cheaply from abroad. Centralised economic planning and production, similarly, can crowd out private investment and enterprise, and nurture deep political inequalities.

Arguably, indeed, the biggest threat to international equality is often government itself. For example, arbitrary and excessive regulations on small businesses, badly performing state schools, high taxes that dampen incentives, public debt and patronage can all hold countries back. Foreign governments may not help either: many poorer countries that are dependent on single crops such as sugar or coffee find their goods priced out of rich markets such

as America and the European Union because of high pro-
tectionist trade barriers.

Capital accumulation. Just as critical is the accumulation
of capital. Capital goods, such as factories and machines,
enable communities to produce far greater output, using
much less effort, than they otherwise could. Around 250
years ago, the Industrial Revolution was built on this simple idea, sparking a self-reinforcing cycle of prosperity in
the advanced countries.

Though today's developing countries are mostly pursuing a similar strategy, they have had less time to build
up their wealth and capital (including human capital: access to quality education requires investment, but greatly
boosts a country's productivity). Some, such as several
sub-Saharan countries, wasted time unproductively by
pursuing other strategies such as state socialism, but are
now on a similar path.

However, building up capital is a long and difficult process; after all, it took the developed countries around 250
years to get to where they are now (and arguably the process began before that, with the creation of liberal institutions including the rule of law, civil and political rights,
education and a widening appreciation of the benefits of
commerce). A better long-term strategy than trying to
equalise countries, therefore, may be to help them acceler-
ate the capital accumulation process.

A young world. Remember too that people tend to accumulate wealth over their life cycles; and half the world's

population are under 30 years old. In much of sub-Saharan Africa, half the population are under 20 years old. In most developed countries, by contrast, half are over 40. So the individual citizens of the developed countries have simply had more time to build up their own human and physical capital. That again contributes to the current inequality between old and rich countries and young and poor ones. But over time, improving healthcare, education, capital accumulation and time should erode it.

Equality, poverty and growth

As policy researcher Tim Worstall pointed out in 2019, the IMF believes there is a Gini 'sweet spot' – that some inequality helps countries grow richer, while too much hits their economic growth. This sounds plausible, except the IMF's sweet spot represents only a little more equality than now exists in the (supposedly very unequal) US, about as much as in the UK, and much less than in France and Sweden. This suggests that poor countries would gain from internal redistribution, but richer countries would harm themselves by it.

But then the IMF may have cause and effect the wrong way round. It is hard to see why greater equality might boost economic growth. It is easier to imagine why rapid growth might raise inequality: simply, entrepreneurs' incomes surge ahead of others' as they grasp the new opportunities that are opening up.

Progress on poverty. It is also hard to believe claims that the world's poor are getting poorer when the worst poverty (accepted as having to live on $1.90 a day or less) has been shrinking so fast. As Johan Norberg notes in his 2016 book *Progress*, on average over the last 25 years, nearly a million people a week have been lifted out of $1.90 a day poverty. In 1950, roughly two-thirds of the world population lived on $1.90 a day or less. In 1980, when globalisation and trade started to expand rapidly, it was around two-fifths. By 1990, that had fallen to just over a third. Now it is one in ten (all figures allowing for inflation).

Figure 2   World population living in extreme poverty, 1820 to 2015

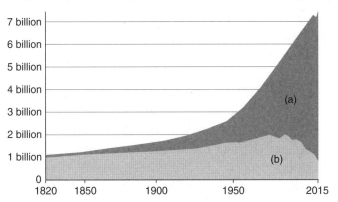

Source: Roser and Ortiz-Ospina (2013); Ravallion (2016) updated with World Bank (2019).

Notes: (a) Number of people *not* living in extreme poverty.
(b) Number of people living in extreme poverty. See Hasell and Roser (2019) for the strengths and limitations of this data and how historians arrive at these estimates.

And that is despite a growing world population: the 1990 $1.90 poverty figure represented nearly 1.9 billion people. And because the world population has grown by a third since then, we might expect $1.90 a day poverty to be a little over 2.5 billion people by now. In fact, it is down to 700 million, mostly in sub-Saharan Africa. Even then, it is concentrated in Nigeria, Congo, Equatorial Guinea, South Sudan, Tanzania, Ethiopia and Madagascar – mostly socialist countries that are not well integrated into the world trading system. Elsewhere, it has mostly disappeared. All in all, $1.90 a day poverty does not seem long for this world.

In fact, trade and globalisation – reinforced with the liberal democratic institutions that make them possible – seem to be the best antidotes to both poverty and inequality. One need only look at post-war East and West Germany, or North and South Korea today, to see the wealth created and spread in more market-oriented economies and the poverty, inequality and hierarchies of socialist autocracies. As Professor Philip Booth and Ben Southwood noted in 2017, the average wage in Vietnam was just $100 per annum in the early 1980s, before globalisation opportunities boosted it to 20 times that amount; the average in China, now a huge exporter, has risen more like 35 times. Our more interconnected and interdependent world is getting both more equal and wealthier too.

6 MUST THE RICH GET RICHER?

In *Capital in the Twenty-First Century*, the French economist Thomas Piketty (2017) argues that returns from wealth are always greater than the general rate of economic growth (or, as he puts it, $r > g$). Accordingly, capital owners accumulate wealth faster than ordinary workers. This, he says, deepens and perpetuates the rich–poor divide, creating an aristocracy of rentiers with an increasing share of total wealth.

Why then, after 300 years of relatively free markets, has this capital-owning aristocracy not already accumulated the world's entire wealth? Piketty responds that capital is periodically dissipated by wars – but then the process starts over again. So, to control the accumulation of capital-based wealth, he suggests a graduated global wealth tax, rising up to 80 per cent on the wealthiest, along with higher inheritance taxes.

Wealth is precarious

Piketty's critics complain that war is only one of many factors that conspire against the accumulation – and retention – of capital. To produce any return at all, capital must be created, grown, managed, maintained and wisely applied. Its owners can fail at any of those stages, and often do. Even if people succeed in building a fortune, they or their heirs can easily lose it again through mistakes, miscalculations and misfortunes. Indeed, a 2015 study by Robert Arnott and colleagues suggests that half of inherited family wealth is lost within about ten years. Family fortunes rise and fall, and few people remain on the *Sunday Times Rich List* or the *Forbes Billionaires List* very long.

Wealth can also be lost by consuming it – in other words, spending and enjoying it – rather than constantly reinvesting it. And also (such as Jamsetji Tata, Bill Gates, George Soros, Andrew Carnegie and the Sainsbury and Weston families) by giving it away to philanthropic causes. Yet Piketty seems to imagine that capital will effortlessly carry on producing growth-beating returns that enrich its owners, like fruit falling off a tree that somehow never needs watering, pruning, pest control or propagation.

Every capital investment carries risk – a word hardly mentioned in Piketty's book, and then only in passing. Products and companies may fail, or succumb to fast-growing competitors, leaving their backers with low-yielding or worthless investments. Risk makes it hard to predict the returns on capital in ten years' time, never mind a hundred; and even a small risk negates Piketty's $r > g$. In the Western economies, returns on capital have been falling since the early 1980s, and risk makes returns even more precarious.

Other forms of wealth

Remember too that capital owners and workers are not separate groups. Workers invest in pension and savings plans, giving them capital holdings of their own. And Piketty overlooks the most important and widely shared form of capital, namely human capital. This, as already explained, is something we all own and invest in – acquiring skills, going to college, learning languages, moving to better jobs and so on. In terms of payback, it is probably the best investment any of us could make. But it is not the preserve of an already wealthy few: we all have it or can acquire it.

One needs only to look at the success of poor immigrant groups to see how people without physical or financial capital, but who are prepared to invest in their human capital, can and do prosper. A quarter of Britain's top 1 per cent of earners are immigrants, as are over a third of FTSE 100 chief executives; a fifth of America's top Fortune 500 companies were founded by immigrants, another fifth by the children of immigrants. True, some of those may be wealthy people moving between countries. But enough of them are poverty-to-prosperity stories to show that you do not need to start financially rich to get financially rich.

Prosperity without equality

Piketty talks approvingly of the nineteenth-century 'Gilded Age' in which incomes accelerated – though at that time there were no laws protecting trade unions, no minimum wage, no welfare state, nor many of the other things that are commonly imagined to bolster equality. But then inventions such as electricity, telegraphs, typewriters and sewing machines drove up industrial productivity, which brought wage rises, shorter working hours and greater spending power, from which all economic groups benefited, particularly the poorest. His claim that 'the poorer half of the population are as poor today as they were in the past, with barely 5 percent of total wealth in 2010, just as in 1910' completely ignores the fact that soaring productivity has made *everyone* much, much richer than they were in 1910. Likewise, the 'Great Compression' of incomes, particularly in America, after World War II was not the happy product of pro-union laws or an expanding welfare state, but of rising post-war trade.

If you want to make a country poor, Piketty's redistributionist policies are a good strategy. Countries who penalise capital owners inevitably make it less worthwhile for people to create, accumulate, preserve and invest capital. They have less domestic and foreign investment and fewer savers to fund production projects. Their focus on distribution rather than growth results in lower growth, productivity and prosperity, which hurts the poor hardest.

7 QUESTIONING THE MORAL CASE

As well as the economic arguments for equality, there are moral arguments too. They may rest on the idea that the equality principle *derives from higher values* such as our universal humanity; or that equality is a *good in itself* because it is just or fair; or that it *delivers other values* such as trust and social harmony. Let us look at each of these.

The universal humanity argument

The *universal humanity* case for equality is that, in all important respects, human beings are alike. They have a similar *identity*, which implies that they are essentially equal and so should be treated equally.

There are problems with this suggestion. For a start, we cannot infer equality from identity. The numbers 3 and 5 share the identity that they are both integers. But they are not equal; and nor can we make them so. Though people speak glibly of humans being 'born equal', the plain reality is that they are not. They differ naturally in many ways – physical, intellectual and moral. To appeal to universal humanity to justify the equalisation of any particular feature, we would have to prove why that should trump all others as the essential mark of human identity. This is not a test that wealth or income would pass.

Some critics also argue that, even if the natural state of human beings is equality, that state is still not necessarily moral, desirable or sustainable. It could be a state where life is 'solitary, poor, nasty, brutish and short,' as the philosopher Thomas Hobbes (1651) put it. Such critics would argue that an unequal society might produce better results. Again, one would have to demonstrate that this is so before the inborn equality argument would have any weight.

Other forms of humanity. It is important to remember that the differences we see in income or wealth are not anyone's conscious choice. They are merely the outcome of impersonal economic processes. And if we *were* trying consciously to allocate incomes based on our shared humanity, would *equality* be our ambition anyway? Perhaps a better indicator of our humanity would be our minimal treatment of others – resolving not to harm others, for example, and providing a 'safety net' for the most unfortunate. It might mean giving others their *due* consideration and respect as fellow humans, but not necessarily *equal* consideration and respect.

Indeed, there may be greater consideration and respect in *unequal* societies. In economies built on specialisation, we value people economically for their different skills; and we value them differently on other measures, such as their social standing or friendliness or courage. It is probably better that people should be valued, by their peers, on these diverse measures, rather than being valued by those in authority on the strength of one single measure. Universal humanity demands we recognise the differences between people, not just their similarities; and that we treat people as individuals, not on the basis of one abstraction such as income or wealth. Given that free individuals have different ambitions, including non-financial ones, it is inevitable that income and wealth inequalities will arise between them. But these are not the ultimate characteristics that define humanity.

John Rawls: equality and fairness

Perhaps the most accomplished attempt to provide a rational moral case for economic equalisation is *A Theory of Justice* by John Rawls. His method is a thought experiment: if we had to design a society, but (from behind a 'veil of ignorance') we did not know what our place in it would be, what kind of a distribution would we design? His answer is that we would exercise caution and choose a relatively equal society with a strong safety net to support the least favoured.

Prospects, not equality. That may be a natural choice for an academic; but academics are notoriously risk-averse. Others have diverse responses to risk and may well place different bets in this gamble. Many may be perfectly willing to take the chance of 'making it big' and ending up better off in a less equal society.

Mathematically, a rational gambler would choose to have a minimum safety net, but not equality. And different sorts of society would give gamblers the same mathematical *expected value* of their choices – so there is nothing uniquely rational about the equality option anyway.

But if the gamblers could decide the *amount* of wealth or income that the society would have, and not just its distribution, they may well decide to have a rich, growing but less equal one rather than a poor, stagnant but more equal one. Or they may choose a less equal but mobile society, believing that this would raise incentives and boost progress and prosperity. Or they might choose a society that was unequal economically but equal in other ways, such as social status. Unfortunately, Rawls's scenario does not allow such possibilities, effectively ruling out everything but economic equality.

Selective information. Rawls also assumes that the gamblers share a 'natural equality', so that they must make their choice on rational grounds rather than on any expectation that they could use their particular powers or abilities to restructure the chosen society in ways that suit them better. And he thinks that this means they would only choose an unequal society if everyone benefited from it. But this supposed 'natural equality' automatically assumes away the very human differences that in reality shape societies. Able and ambitious people, for example, would have no reason to choose equality; they might prefer an unequal society where they could elbow their way to the top.

The gamblers must plainly have some familiarity with how societies function in order to know what they are betting on; but not so much that they can be confident of ending up better off than others. Rawls presumes they all understand the principle of *justice*, but since he defines this as *fairness*, this inevitably pushes their choices towards equality, rather than other possibilities such as diversity or mobility. In other words, he designs his gamblers and their gamble in ways that necessarily support the equality case, overriding all the other aspects of society such as family or merit or liberty. Indeed, there is little mention of liberty and its value in *A Theory of Justice*. And while family and upbringing are obviously a major source of inequality, Rawls draws back from excising it from his supposedly rational, equal society.

Serving or deserving. However much we equalise wealth and incomes, we are still left with the fact that other human differences leave us unequal in many different ways. To restore equality, Rawls proposes that those with natural talents should use them only for the common good, not their own advancement. But while such natural endowments are a matter of luck, that does not mean that they are 'not deserved' and should thus be given up. Personal achievement is almost always rooted in some natural quality, such as fitness or skill; but we still think that athletes 'deserve' their medals, and do not imagine that other people have any entitlement to them.

In sum, Rawls's argument, though highly influential, is unsatisfactory. Justice does not mean only fairness; much less does it mean equality. A just society is one that respects people as individuals, tolerates their differences, secures their freedom, protects their rights, and minimises coercion upon them. If we start with a preconceived notion of an equal society, we cannot guarantee any of those outcomes.

8   QUESTIONING THE PRACTICAL CLAIMS

It is questionable, then, how far equality can be judged as a moral good in itself, or one that stems from fundamental values such as justice. And there are also doubts about how far equality helps us achieve other values too.

Errors of *The Spirit Level*

The thesis of *The Spirit Level* by Kate Pickett and Richard G. Wilkinson (2010) is that nearly all social problems, from unhappiness to obesity, mental illness, infant mortality, bad schools and murder rates, are linked to income inequality. These problems, the authors suggest, may be a result of the psychological damage provoked by inequality, such as envy, distrust and greed. To prove their thesis, they rank different countries in terms of their inequality and then rate them on various measures, finding a correlation in nearly every case. Even though correlation and causation are two different things, their evidence has still convinced thousands of readers that inequality does indeed cause a wide array of social problems.

However, many critics take strong issue with the book's thesis, method and findings, not to mention the popular conclusions based on them. For example, the prominent UK economist John Kay points out that most of the alleged correlations are presented as scattergrams with a 'trend line' drawn through them. But in almost every case there are so many 'outlier' countries (and often, so few 'inliers') that without the trend line, the data look more like a completely random scatter.

Cherry-picked data. In *The Spirit Level Delusion*, Christopher Snowdon (2010) argues that the choice of which countries are included or excluded makes a huge difference to the findings and can neutralise or even reverse the supposed correlations. The *Spirit Level* authors claim that there are good reasons for their choices, and that they have to restrict themselves to large countries that collect the data that they are evaluating in each case, but Snowdon argues that some measures (such as life expectancy) are highly sensitive to what countries are included, and that the omissions of Singapore, South Korea, Hong Kong and the Czech Republic, plus the sporadic exclusion of other countries that may not fit the narrative, amount to 'cherry picking'.

Complex causes. It is unlikely that between-country differences in health, crime or other measures could stem from inequality alone, says Snowdon. Poor health, for example, is more likely to be down to poverty, poor housing, bad education, long hours in manual or agricultural labour, and even the age profile of the country concerned. Infant mortality rates may be more plausibly linked to differences in marriage ages, medicines and data collection than inequality, and infant mortality is now so rare in advanced countries that any differences are irrelevant (though for what it's worth, Singapore – a highly unequal society – has the world's lowest rates).

Obesity, another supposed correlation, is more likely to reflect different countries' diet and lifestyle traditions rather than inequality. Divergent rates of tobacco and alcohol consumption may be influenced by the size of the taxes levied on these products. Mental illness rates, too, may have many causes other than the supposed anguish provoked by inequality. Many poorer countries do not even have data on mental disorders, while richer ones that can afford more psychiatrists naturally see more patients diagnosed.

The same complex causes apply elsewhere to other *Spirit Level* correlations. The authors argue that relatively unequal societies such as the US send more people to prison, suggesting that inequality provokes crime. But that difference seems to be more about punishment cultures than crime rates, says Snowdon, since some relatively equal countries have high violent crime rates but choose to send fewer people to prison. Again, high rates of recycling in Japan and Sweden may not show that such highly equal societies have greater social commitment, simply that recycling is compulsory in those places. A better index of social commitment might in fact be the world-beating philanthropic giving in America.

Impossible measurements. Perhaps the most difficult phenomenon to pin down is the alleged correlation between equality and happiness, which is notoriously difficult (and arguably impossible) to measure. For example, Finland, despite its constant concerns about neighbouring Russia, is rated as the world's happiest country; but that might be a consequence of its small size and homogeneity, which probably promotes trust and confidence; or even that two-thirds of the population are Lutherans, whose church teaches contentment with one's lot. And if happiness measures tell us anything, it is that people in rich countries are generally happier than those in poor ones, regardless of income inequalities. Indeed, extensive polling by researchers Jonathan Kelley and Mariah Evans (2017) debunks the idea that inequality undermines happiness: in developing countries, inequality is seen as an indicator of opportunity and upward mobility; in developed countries, there seems to be no relationship at all.

The suggestion that inequality breeds envy and social tension is questionable too. Again, it is hard to measure either notion; what should count as indicators of social tension is a matter of opinion – civil wars, coups, riots, aggressive social media posts? And, over history, wars and uprisings have happened for many varied reasons, not necessarily just internal social tensions. Arguably, inequality was far greater centuries ago, but there was less envy; or perhaps more acceptance that inequality was a normal condition. And those who foment political turmoil may have many motives other than envy.

Misdirecting our focus

By comparing a large array of social measures against inequality, *The Spirit Level* forces us into a tunnel vision that inequality is the crucial factor, even though the data are unreliable, the measures questionable, and the reality very complicated.

What data there are come from a wide group of countries with diverse populations and different values, cultures, religions, ethnicities, histories, traditions, diets, educational standards, welfare states and family structures. Norway, South Korea, Israel, Switzerland or Brunei are all wealthy countries but have very little else in common. Income inequality does not explain Asia's low teenage birth rate, Americans' obesity and philanthropy, Japan's high suicide rate, or the high levels of trust in Scandinavia. There is simply no reliable evidence, nor academic agreement, that inequality has the many undesirable results of which it is accused.

9 EQUAL PAY IN THE WORKPLACE

The contradictions of equal pay

The problem of how to establish equal but fair pay in the workplace crystallises the wider problems of turning the equality idea into practice.

Equal pay contradictions. Let us start with an extreme case, where employers are obliged to give their workers equal wages. If employees work different hours, perhaps due to illness or family commitments or even the bad timekeeping of some, those groups would end up with more per hour worked than others. This inevitably leads to conflicts among the workforce, as CEOs who have tried equal pay policies voluntarily (such as Simon Benton of UK psychotherapy company Spill) have discovered to their cost. The result is unhappy workplaces and falling productivity.

Perhaps that is why not even socialist countries have equal pay rates, and why campaigners usually call for 'more equality' – maximum ratios between higher and lower earners, minimum and maximum wages, and so on – rather than simply 'equality'. However, the same problems arise under such policies, even if in more dilute form.

Non-monetary factors. Also, an equal pay policy does not recognise the many dissimilarities between different jobs. Some are pleasant, some not; some come with 'perks' while others do not; some will require a large initial investment of time and effort on training before a person can even start on them. Why should anyone agree to do a job that required considerable investment, for the same pay as a job that anyone could walk straight in to?

If we were to stretch the meaning of 'equal pay' and try to compensate people for these differences in jobs, how could we possibly calculate their value? That exists only in the minds of the individuals concerned. And if we wanted to compensate people for doing difficult jobs, does that mean we will pay skilled workers less, because skilled workers find the same job easier?

Unequal families. Another problem is that employees might have families of different sizes. With equal pay, a single-person household would end up better off than one with two people but only one earner, and very much better than a family of four or five. Paying people equally, therefore, still does not mean that everyone becomes equally well off.

Different ways of acting. Workers might be given equal incomes, but some may choose to save and invest more than others or pass money on to their families. There is no injustice in this – it does not injure anyone else – and indeed we generally regard such prudence and responsibility as laudable. But it means that, despite paying people equally, some families and individuals end up much better off than others.

The same happens when people have equal incomes, but their consumption is different. Some, for example, may need expensive medical care or repairs to their home. Others may choose to spend on designer clothes or a family wedding. Yet others may simply squander their earnings, leaving them badly off. Whatever the reason, the result is that, despite their equal pay, they each end up with different amounts of money.

Is there a gender pay gap?

It is routinely asserted that there is a 'gender gap' between how men and women are paid for similar work, which is taken as a sign of discrimination and unfairness. Critics point to differences in average wage rates between men and women, which in some developed countries are as high as 40 per cent. And in many countries, few of the top earners are women. In response, the politicians of several countries demand that larger firms publish their pay rates for males and females and set about equalising them.

A narrowing gap. However, there is good evidence that (in the advanced countries at least) there is currently no significant gender gap, and that policies based on it are ill-founded. There is certainly a gender gap between *older* workers, but that is because those people began work some decades ago, a time of discrimination and large gender pay gaps; and when employees got annual increases, those pay gaps persisted. But those entering the workforce today are more likely to be paid equally. For the under-thirties, the gap has largely faded (and in some countries, such as the US, documented by the Pew Research Center in 2013, it has almost wholly disappeared).

Origins of the gap. There is still a pay gap, but most of it is a *caring* gap rather than a gender gap, because women much more often take the lead in raising children and looking after relatives. (In the UK, for example, around two-thirds of carers are women, according to the IZA Institute of Labor Economics, and estimates from the OECD and others suggest a similar predominance across a range of countries.) Because of this, women may be more likely to seek flexible or part-time working. But part-time and flexible workers are of less value to employers because they cost more to manage and may not be on hand when needed. Consequently, many women with caring responsibilities settle for lower pay or lower-grade jobs in which flexible hours cause employers fewer problems.

Women may well start work on the same pay and same upward trajectory as men. But those who in their twenties and thirties take years off work or work reduced hours to raise children will fall behind – significantly behind – on that lifetime progression. When they resume work, their pay generally rises again but (since pay reflects experience and years of service) they re-start from a lower absolute level than the full-timers have by then achieved.

Other explanations. And there are other reasons. High marginal tax rates and generous social benefits may induce women with caring responsibilities to stay off work for longer, leaving them even further behind. There may be gender differences in temperament: in the US, Pew Center research suggests that women prefer jobs they enjoy, that offer security, and allow them to take off time for caring responsibilities, while men are more willing to climb the greasy pole to promotion and advancement.

Women might also be less aggressive in pay bargaining (corroborated by the fact that there is a smaller wage gap where collective bargaining prevails). In cultures where women customarily take partners who are older, and therefore already advanced on the pay progression, they may be more willing to accept lower pay rises. In addition, women may have different work preferences, more often taking jobs in small companies or in non-profit bodies, and jobs that are more pleasant and less risky, all of which are by their nature less well paid.

Statistical errors. The raw statistics can also be misleading. It is wrong to compare *mean* wages, for example, as the distribution of incomes is so skewed. While there is a lower limit (such as statutory minimum wages) to what people will or can work for, there is no upper limit on pay. And many more women, as we have seen, choose flexible or part-time (but lower-paid) jobs. One or two male billionaires can therefore widen the gender *averages* considerably. To understand the situation of most ordinary people, we should look instead at the *median* wage, where there are equal numbers of people above and below. There, we find much less of a gender difference.

Natural differences. Given all this, it seems that for the most part – perhaps nearly all, according to some studies – the supposed gender pay gap is not due to discrimination or unfairness but to the natural lifestyle choices of women and men. Governments might seek to rebalance these differences with policies such as free childcare, or retraining programmes for women who have taken time off to care for children, or other measures. But unless there is a social revolution in gender attitudes to work and caring, this difference seems likely to remain.

Are CEOs worth their money?

Early January brings annual complaints that the CEOs in FTSE or Dow Jones companies have now earned more than their average workers earn in a year. This is claimed to be grossly unfair – CEOs may work long hours, but not *that much* longer than other workers – and is accompanied by proposals to curb this unfairness by imposing a 'maximum wage' (reflecting, at the top end, the 'minimum wage' at the other) or a limit on the ratio of the pay of executives to the pay of the lowest-paid company employees.

Unequal attitudes. By contrast, very few people would regard it as unfair that leading artists, actors, racing drivers or football players earn very large salaries. They make a big difference to the lives of many people, sometimes millions, who voluntarily pay them for the pleasure. But then CEOs make a big difference to their many shareholders, who also voluntarily pay them for the wealth they create. A good CEO can boost the value of a company hugely; a bad one can bring it (and its investors) to bankruptcy. Yet it is suggested that company shareholders should be forbidden from paying what they think a successful CEO is worth to them and to everyone working in their company.

Adding value. CEO pay is certainly high and has increased. But then with globalisation, the top companies in the leading stock markets have also grown, in size, complexity and international footprint. There are few people with the skills to manage such large and complex international enterprises, just as there are few world-beating sports personalities. Accordingly, there is increasing competition for CEO talent, and it is no surprise that the pay of both CEOs and sports stars is high.

Who decides? Critics may argue that executive pay is *too* high, but who has the right to decide? The only objective way to judge what CEOs are worth is after the event – to see how their arrival or departure affects the company's share price. And that, as policy analyst Sam Bowman pointed out in 2016, can be very considerably indeed. Apple, for example, lost 5 per cent of its value (about $17.5 billion) when founder and CEO Steve Jobs died. Microsoft's value rose 8 per cent ($20 billion) after Steve Balmer's 2013 resignation. In the same year, Angela Ahrendt's departure from Burberry reduced the value of firm by more than £500 million. These are big numbers, all down to single individuals.

A CEO's job is hard to price. It is not like piecework, where pay reflects the number of widgets produced; it requires vision and presence and flair. Shareholders could fire CEOs or cut their pay if they thought they were getting poor returns on the money; and sometimes they do. But mostly they are happy to endorse the pay packages of their CEOs. Who is to say they are wrong? But inequality critics would gainsay their valuation, backed up by legislative force.

10 THE ROOTS OF EQUALISATION POLICY

From ethics to politics

Further problems arise when moral ideas, backed by questionable statistics, morph into political programmes. Moral ideas are about how we would *like* people to be; political policies *force* them to be something. That is a big difference.

False assumptions. Our natural, cultural and religious feelings of fairness lead many people to assume that equality is the only moral situation; and too often they rely on questionable statistics and loaded terms to reinforce that assumption. And since private charity (focused on poverty, not equality) is not up to the job of equalising everyone, the further presumption is that government must do it, by force.

Underlying this is a presumption that individuals are not responsible for their economic position; that inequality is created by society; and that the poor are victims of circumstance while the rich are undeserving manipulators. But this narrative overlooks the importance of factors such as hard work, ambition, skill-acquisition, willpower and resilience in determining where people end up in terms of incomes and wealth.

Justifying redistribution. To some academics, the equality narrative provides the justification (or possibly the veneer) for moving from ethical thought to political action. To governments, it suggests a way to defuse people's envy and provides the grounds for political intervention.

Hence the demands for a political programme to equalise any differences that do not actively promote the collective good. That treats humans in depersonalised terms, as if they exist only to serve some social end, selected by the authorities. And it makes ethical ideas (about how we live our lives) serve political ideas (about how we should serve others). But ethics should inform politics, not the other way round.

The impossibility of equal outcomes

Non-material differences. In the rush to turn the moral idea of economic equality into political policy, we forget that human beings do not just *have* things: they create and cherish things, including their many *non-financial* ambitions. And they differ in countless ways, mostly harmless – or even beneficial: perhaps, like the benefits of biodiversity, our society is made more secure by our diversity too.

Many other differences, like those in ability or upbringing, we cannot change. Nor compensate: how would we judge the financial value of a stimulating childhood, or the cost of extreme shyness? How would we measure joy and sadness, and give people an equal measure of both? But then human satisfaction comes from meeting our own internal goals, not from our outward wealth.

We cannot equalise these things because we cannot put prices on them; so people focus instead on what we *can* measure and manipulate – income and wealth. It seems at best a very partial approach, at worst a highly distorting one. And even this is inadequate: we can hope to equalise wealth and incomes, but that is no guarantee that people end up with equal benefit.

The rockstar problem. Then there is the rockstar problem. Even if everyone starts from a position of complete equality, fans will willingly pay money to see their favourite rockstar in concert. They each end the evening a little poorer and the rockstar ends it a lot richer. To maintain the equality that we started with would require constant reassessment and redistribution of incomes. But since the transactions were entirely voluntary, no harm or injustice has been done to anyone. So on what grounds could we reverse this voluntary exchange, other than some authority's social vision?

Moreover, those of us who are poor guitar players are hardly equal to any rockstar, either in our ability or our earning power. We could perhaps even things up by cutting off one or two of the best guitar players' fingers. Apart from denying ourselves some amazing musical performances, this would be an act of violence against them. But then all forced equalisation, whether of guitarists or earners, requires the threat of violence against some people.

It also raises a contradiction in that it requires people to be treated *unequally* to produce the intended equality. The narrative assumes that such forced, unequal treatment in the name of equalisation does not conflict with other parts of life, such as justice, civil rights, freedom, family, prosperity and the elimination of poverty. But it does.

Compensating bad luck

Given the impossibility of achieving equal outcomes, a common suggestion is that we should at least compensate people for bad luck. That might mean compensation for 'brute' luck, such as being born into an uncaring family, going blind, being robbed, or other misfortunes beyond the victim's control.

But, apart from the usual problem of how to measure the burden of this bad luck and decide what compensation is appropriate, such a policy is complicated by the fact that there are many different sorts of luck that affect all human life in different ways and to different degrees in different mixtures. It is not obvious how to unscramble that and decide what we should compensate, to what extent, and what we should not.

Brute luck and option luck. Alongside the 'brute luck' of things beyond the individual's control there is 'option luck' – how people's deliberate, calculated gambles turn out. Examples might include buying a winning lottery ticket or investing in a business that goes bankrupt. There is some agreement on the merits of compensating brute luck (though liberals would say that, where possible, people should insure against it rather than expect taxpayers to bail them out). But there is no agreement on what to do about option luck.

One argument is that we should not compensate option luck at all, because to do so will extinguish personal responsibility and induce people to take absurd risks. They would know that they could undertake highly uncertain business ventures or gamble away their home on a game of cards, or damage their health by abusing drugs, knowing that their loss or injury would be fully compensated. But this policy produces harsh and inconsistent outcomes. We may well baulk at compensating people who gamble at cards, but simple humanity would demand we help a motorcyclist who suffered head injuries through not wearing a helmet. Where we draw the line is a subjective choice. And again, liberals might say that voluntary aid to victims of bad option luck is fine, but forcing others to help by paying higher taxes is not.

Most of life's outcomes are a mixture of different kinds of luck, circumstance, judgement, effort, application and much else. Even limiting things to brute luck and option luck, it is rarely obvious how much of either is responsible for any outcome. Many people smoke cigarettes, for example, but only some contract lung cancer. Many people are born into well-off, caring and stimulating households that provide a springboard into education and business, but only a tiny few become billionaires. How can we determine how much of someone's success was due to a helpful upbringing, and how much due to their hard work, diligence and other things in their control? Indeed, is their diligence wholly within their own control, or mainly the result of their upbringing? And were their choices successful because of the brute luck of being in the right place at the right time? Once again, an equalisation policy that initially looks straightforward turns out not to be so.

11 POLITICAL APPROACHES TO EQUALISATION

From equality to equity

If complete equalisation is impossible, and compensating people for bad luck is problematic, how much equalisation should we aim for? There are many options, but none of them really solves the problem because each is consistent with a hierarchical outcome, not just an equal one.

Theoretical strategies. A classical liberal, for example, would argue for *equal political and legal rights* and otherwise to leave people equally alone. But that still subjectively places the equalisation of those rights above the equalisation of other things such as income, wealth or social status. A second liberal option is simply to give people *equal concern and respect*. But what does that mean, and what do we do about people who demand *more* respect and status than is given to others? A third possibility is to accept that there are many differences between people but to *treat similar cases similarly* – rewarding virtue and punishing crime, say. But that still leaves us with countless other uncompensated inequalities.

A fourth strategy, proposed by the Nobel economist Amartya Sen, is to try to *equalise capabilities*, such that everyone has access to the basic resources (e.g. food, shelter and education) that they need to pursue fulfilling lives. Yet even this could leave *outcomes* very unequal. Also, there is no clear way to measure 'capabilities' or know if we have equalised them. And what counts as 'basic' resources is a matter of opinion. Though Sen's approach helpfully makes us focus on our minimal treatment of other human beings, the specific policies built on it are bound to be controversial.

Addressing people's needs

Diverse needs. Another strategy is to try to equalise people according to need – along the lines of Karl Marx's famous dictum, 'From each according to his ability, to each according to his needs.' But unless 'need' means only the minimum needed for life, what counts as 'need' is again subjective. How can we know, for example, if people 'need' a bigger house or better clothes? Some people might feel a burning 'need' for revenge, or narcotics, or social status. Should we gratify these questionable 'needs'?

Providing equal material goods. The needs approach draws us into the idea that instead of impotently trying to equalise incomes, we should instead provide people with the same bundle of material goods – equal schools, healthcare, housing, food, transport and so on. Yet such 'universal basic services' would not equalise the benefits that people enjoy. Free education is of no value to those without children to benefit from it; sick people need more healthcare; identical housing would not suit large families; manual workers need more calorific food than office workers; and those who work from home need less transport than do commuters. Supporters argue that providing universal basic services is fair because people take them up according to their needs. But ignoring individual differences seems likely to produce constant complaints of unfairness.

Dangers of these approaches. The 'needs' and 'universal basic services' strategies imply a huge state control over production and distribution. They would require a state apparatus, and taxation to fund it, much greater than any that now exist. And they would put enormous power, discretion and patronage into the hands of politicians and administrators (which is hardly 'equality'). Moreover, the state monopoly provision of so many fundamental goods would stifle innovation, progress and economic growth. We could of course provide equal access to these goods by having them privately produced while giving people ration cards; but deciding who gets access to what rations is still a huge source of power over others.

Contribution to society. Another problem for these two approaches is that even shirkers who consciously evade work and effort would still be entitled to the same goods. Hence another suggestion: that people should be rewarded only in proportion to their contribution to society. Arguably the market economy already does this: in general, people get paid according to the value they deliver to others. But that still leaves us with wide disparities between, say, IT entrepreneurs whose products enhance the lives of millions and a part-time cleaner in a small café. And without market prices, we have no way to measure people's 'contribution to society'. What should be the relative rewards going to a nurse, a judge, a deep-sea diver, a tax inspector or the inventor of life-saving medicines, say? There would be constant disputes, with different groups arguing that they contributed more than others, and no way to resolve them.

Narrowing the differences

Given all these problems, the intellectual debate inevitably elides from greater *equality* of wealth and incomes to greater *equity* – what differences in wealth and incomes are still acceptable. The focus here is on ending sharp differences in wealth, income or other characteristics.

Problems in the approach. But this pragmatic approach is not robust: if inequality is considered bad, mitigated inequality is still not good. Nor is the approach a stable one: we might aim to keep inequality within 'fair' limits, but fairness is a subjective idea, and there would be disagreement about how much inequality was acceptable. Quite probably, *more equal* incomes or wealth would cause even greater argument than fully equalised ones, with people still envious of others who were left better off, and complaining that their special needs or contributions have not been recognised.

Given all these problems, it is no surprise that the debate then moves on to the question of whether, rather than equalising or even narrowing outcomes, we can equalise or narrow the *opportunities* that are available to everyone.

12 EQUALITY OF OPPORTUNITY

Equality of opportunity is the idea that everyone should compete on equal terms for jobs, civil offices or other opportunities, regardless of their wealth, upbringing or other characteristics such as race, religion, gender or age. Only *relevant* characteristics, such as their ability to do the job, should count.

One of the biggest factors that might bar people from accessing advantageous jobs and opportunities is of course upbringing. Children from stable, loving, stimulating families are better placed to do well at school and go on to college or train for a well-paid profession. Therefore, much of the equality of opportunity discussion is about how we can equalise, or at least narrow, these background differences.

Once again, there are shortcomings to this. For example, focusing on equal opportunity for advantageous jobs and offices implies that inequalities in income and status remain with us. The approach seems to accept the idea of a meritocratic society, with all the inequalities that implies, not an equal one. And we are again singling out just one small part of human life, namely upbringing, and ignoring the rest.

The meaning of equal opportunity

Impossibility of equal upbringing. Plainly, the family is a powerful generator and reinforcer of inequality. The fact that upbringing could seriously affect people's future lives makes us ask how it could be equalised such that everyone has a fair opportunity to attain any position for which they are qualified.

Education, in particular, could make a big difference to life outcomes, but access to the best schools, and educational attainment, may depend on upbringing too. We could establish a state education monopoly to ensure equality in schooling, but even within such a uniform system, some teachers will be more inspirational than others – indeed, that seems to make more difference than how much is spent on education – so there is still no guarantee of equality. And family values will continue to benefit some children as they advance through school and into employment.

Perhaps the only way to equalise all that would be to take children into state nurseries at birth, and indeed minimise any human contact. This is of course an absurd and unjust idea, albeit one that highlights the essential impossibility of equalising opportunities.

Workers and employees. And do job candidates' rights to equal consideration override employers' choices? Suppose (to take a real-world legal case from the 1970s) that someone advertises for a Scottish cook. Perhaps they like Scots, or believe them thrifty and honest, or prefer Scottish food, or love listening to Scottish accents, or any of a hundred other reasons. Should the law stop them from rejecting all French or Italian applicants, whom they perhaps like and trust less? Should their own preferences, even if irrational, count for nothing?

The worry is that, without such legal guarantees of equal opportunity, employers might be able to discriminate against certain groups (religious or ethnic groups perhaps, or immigrants), leaving them permanently excluded and disadvantaged. But immigrants, to take that example, can and do overcome such prejudice by simply accepting lower wages and getting into work – whereupon they can demonstrate their ability and reliability, causing the prejudice against them to dispel.

Plainly, employers must be able to reject candidates if they are not able to do the job. Sadly, this means that unskilled workers, and those with poor literacy, numeracy and language fluency, will be excluded as candidates more often; and minority groups may have more difficulty in finding and applying for jobs. But these groups all tend to be poorer, and equality of opportunity may do little to advance their prospects.

What qualifications count? Who decides what is meant by 'ability to do the job'? Would past criminal convictions justify a candidate being rejected, or only those convictions that seem relevant (such as fraud convictions in the case of people applying for bank jobs)? How serious must the offence have been to exclude someone? And how should we treat candidates who have the technical skills to do the job, but show little motivation, commitment or enthusiasm for the work? Do they still have to be included under an equal opportunities policy?

Such judgements are inherently subjective and perhaps best left to employers – even if it may sometimes be unclear if a candidate is being rejected through inability or because of discrimination.

Should we worry about inheritance?

Different families give their children different starts in many ways, though again the policy focus is on the manipulable ones, income and wealth. But is the inheritance of wealth important, and if so, how can we compensate for it?

Size of the factor. Inheriting wealth might be an advantage, but inheritance in general accounts for only a modest proportion of personal wealth. Even then, inheritance may not raise inequality much, as that depends on the actions of those who inherit. As we have seen, family wealth soon dissipates; and those who inherit a family business may not run it well; and those inheriting financial assets may invest the money unwisely.

In any event, most financial success comes, not from inheritance, but from people's own choices, motivation and application. Two-thirds of the world's richest people have made their own fortunes, not inherited them. In 2021 Ramsey Solutions reported that in a survey of 10,000 American millionaires only a fifth of them had received any inheritance at all, and only 3 per cent had inherited $1 million or more.

Is luck unfair? In any case, why should we penalise people merely for being born to parents who help them, financially or otherwise? They have done nothing wrong, so why penalise their good luck? Most of life is a matter of luck – being in the right place at the right time, meeting useful friends, taking chances that pay off, for example. And bad things happen to people too – for example, their job might fall victim to changing technology. But none of this is *unfair*, something that must be penalised or compensated. It is just happenstance.

Like a lottery prize, inheritance is a matter of luck. We accept that people have a right to their lottery prize, so why not their inheritance?

The money that testators give their heirs does not come to them only as a matter of luck, of course. In general, they have earned it by saving and investing. Most inheritance, though, is not from the vast estates of the super-rich but comes in small amounts within ordinary families. It gives their heirs some security and reduces their reliance on the state – that is, taxpayers.

The rules dominate. The rules on inheritance can make a big difference to outcomes. For example, the British tradition of primogeniture has helped preserve large country estates. There may be good justifications for this tradition: Frances's *egalité* tradition of dividing land between the surviving children, by contrast, creates unviably small farms. If we did want to make outcomes more equal, we might do better to reform the rules around inheritance, rather than trying to redistribute after the fact.

Inheritance taxation damages the economy. It encourages wealth holders to spend rather than save and invest, diminishing the nation's productive capital and thus its productivity and growth. And it encourages them to hold what wealth they have in assets that might escape the worst of the tax, rather than in more productive ones.

Rising equality of opportunity. Though wealth may correlate with the luck of family background or good schooling, it is not entirely *due to* it. Rockstar incomes depend more on natural talent than education or family. The fact that talented people from modest backgrounds do become rockstars – and lawyers, doctors, CEOs and prime ministers – suggests that opportunities are already quite equal, and probably getting more so.

13 REDISTRIBUTION POLICIES

There is even less agreement on what practical policies might best promote greater economic equality than there is over the theory of it. Possible options range from progressive taxation through wealth taxes, increased welfare, minimum wages, negative income taxes and affirmative action to promote disadvantaged groups. But there is a different sort of strategy, less mentioned: promoting economic growth.

Progressive taxation

Progressive taxation is the idea that those on higher earnings should pay a larger percentage of their income in tax than those on lower earnings. This is the usual contradiction – unequal treatment in the name of equality. But supporters justify it on the grounds of *diminishing marginal utility*. Put simply, people who have more of something tend to get less value and enjoyment from it. Having one bottle of water to hand on a hot day might be a boon; a second, welcome; but there is scant benefit in having another 50.

The same is true of income, runs the argument. For a low earner, a single pound or dollar or euro is vital; for a middle earner, important; but for a high earner, a matter of little concern. It is therefore fair to take a higher proportion of high-earners' pay because they will not feel the loss as keenly. That extra revenue will enable us to support low earners and thus equalise incomes more robustly. And in the process, the total utility enjoyed by the community will be raised, because money is being taken from those who value it less and given to those who value it more.

Subjectivity problem. This is of course all subjective. The usefulness or enjoyment that anyone derives from a pound or dollar or euro is in their own mind. We cannot measure it, any more than we can measure people's pleasure or pain, happiness or grief, anxiety or calm. And (like any of these other emotions) we certainly cannot equalise it between one person and another. So we cannot be sure that taking money from some people and giving it to others will raise the total value that society enjoys.

Individuals are diverse, and do not all value income solely for what it buys. Many people may regard income as a mark of achievement, acceptance, success and status. Others may wish to provide for their heirs. Some may be keen to save and start a business. Yet others might want to give all they can to philanthropic causes. These high earners may therefore feel the loss of income nearly as keenly as lower earners.

Limits to majority policy. Even if we believed that progressive taxes would raise the total value in society, does a political majority really have the right to impose such redistribution on the (higher-earning) minority? That would be to treat income as a fixed resource, believing that if some people have wealth, there is less to go round everyone else. This is wrong: value is not fixed but is *created*, through innovation, investment and productivity. That is why the populations of free, developed countries are a hundred times better off than they were in 1800. The great majority of high earners have become so because they deliver value to and improve the lives of thousands or millions of others. And as we have seen, they are already highly taxed.

We cannot separate outcomes from the process that creates them. Progressive taxes inevitably discourage entrepreneurship and investment, and therefore dampen progress and economic growth. That leaves us with the prospect of society becoming more equal, but worse off.

Wealth taxes

Another possible equalisation strategy is to levy an annual tax on the wealth of rich people. Oxfam, for example, proposes a 0.5 per cent tax on wealth, which sounds relatively modest; but in a time of low interest rates, where investments might earn as little as 1 per cent in real terms, that amounts to a 50 per cent tax on investment returns. A bout of inflation would reduce those returns (raising the effective tax rate even higher) or even drive them negative (in which case we would be taxing people on *diminishing* wealth).

Such taxes would plainly change people's behaviour. They might simply spend their wealth, robbing the economy of investment needed for growth. They might try to avoid the tax by moving their money abroad or into untaxed but less productive investments – undermining economic growth again. Or, since wealth is hard to measure, they might simply lie and undervalue the assets they hold. Thomas Piketty's suggestion of a wealth tax of 80 per cent or more would have even more spectacularly counterproductive results.

The variable value of assets. The wealth measurement problem is serious in another way too. A person's wealth is the market price of the assets they own, minus their debts. But market prices rise and fall – often substantially. A billionaire's wealth might come from a company that has developed some highly successful product. But at any time, changes in technology, fashion or resource availability could sink that enterprise and leave its owner bankrupt. The amount of tax payable would depend on which day the tax assessment was made. To take the extreme case, if it were the day before a stock market crash, we would be taxing people who were no longer wealthy, which seems arbitrary and unjust.

Limits to revenues. People also overestimate what wealth taxes can achieve. Booth and Southwood (2017) calculate that if you took the entire wealth of the world's richest people and distributed it equally through the lifetimes of the world population, you would be able to give everyone a pay rise of only $1.35 a year. And you would destroy all incentives.

Oxfam's tax might raise about $200 billion, a tiny fraction of the $22,000 billion that world governments spend, much of it on welfare, pensions and other equalising benefits. Certainly, $200 billion directed to expanding the opportunities available to the world's poorest could achieve much good; but governments have their own domestic problems (and politicians their own pet projects) to focus on, so the chance of that happening is vanishingly small.

Offshore wealth. A common theme of the equality narrative is that rich people escape taxes by parking their wealth offshore in low-tax jurisdictions (denigrated as 'tax havens'), thereby denying money to schools, welfare and other state services. But in fact such wealth is not merely 'parked' – it goes into dedicated financial centres that consolidate, manage and direct it into the most productive uses that can be found. That capital is therefore invested far more productively than if it went in taxation to governments, who consume most of it on current spending, leaving less to invest in the productive future of the country and thereby making people at all income levels worse off.

The possibility of people moving their money – or themselves – to low-tax jurisdictions suggests that to be effective, a wealth tax would have to be global. This would be very difficult to achieve. Many low-tax jurisdictions are small, sometimes island, nations, with little else to sustain them other than capital management. And even larger countries might thwart international agreement if they thought they might gain from having lower taxes or even softer enforcement. The higher the tax, the more people will strive to find ways to escape it. So perhaps a wealth tax, particularly on the scale advocated by Piketty, is simply impractical and pointless to debate.

Minimum wages

Laws forbidding employers from paying people below a certain hourly rate are seen as a way of raising the incomes of the poorest workers, without raising taxes. It is argued that this will raise those workers' motivation, boost investment in productivity, and increase the incentive to get off social benefits and into work.

But minimum wages do not help the poorest. The poorest are not in work at all and (say critics) are priced out of work by the minimum wage policy. Unless workers generate more value for a business than all the costs of employing them (wages, taxes, pensions, management time, etc.), they will not be taken on. Minimum wages therefore see lower-value jobs being phased out or done by robots instead of people. That makes getting a job harder for those we most want to help but who are less valuable to a business, such as inexperienced young people, unskilled workers or immigrants with a poor grasp of the language. Indeed, the fact that there is commonly a lower minimum wage rate for young people seems an admission that they would otherwise be priced out. Though there is some evidence that they in fact are: the loss of 'starter jobs' (cinema ushers, supermarket bag packers, filling station pump attendants, etc.) might leave some young people unable to get on the jobs ladder at all, and dependent on social benefits.

Supporters of minimum wages argue that these job losses arise for different reasons such as technological change, and that there is no clear evidence that minimum wages really do affect employment. But even if that were true, do minimum wages really hit their intended target? In many minimum wage countries, the majority of minimum wage earners do not even come from poor households: they are students living with parents, retired people wanting to keep active, or partners of higher earners who enjoy the comradeship of the workplace. If we really wanted to help the poor, we would do far better with an earned income tax credit or negative income tax system, which would allow employers to pay the wages that the job justified, but which would make up the pay of the genuinely poorest to the acceptable level.

Different standards for different groups

Another way in which we might help poorer people, beyond merely outlawing discrimination, is to compensate groups that are underrepresented in advantageous appointments by applying different standards. This might include quota systems, where a certain proportion of places in a school, or jobs in a business, university or government department, must go to people of particular gender, race or religion.

A problem with this policy is that it focuses on groups, not individuals. Boosting the prospects of a particular group may help its well-off members as well as its poor ones, which is not the intention. Then there is the question of *which* groups deserve special treatment, who should decide this, and on what grounds. There seems no objective answer.

Inconsistent treatment. Skewing opportunities towards some groups, however deserving, imposes costs on a society. If employers are obliged to fill their quotas from chosen groups, even if they are well qualified, professional standards may fall. Also, people who are not in those groups, but who individually may be just as deserving, are denied the same opportunities. And we risk loading irrelevant values onto what should be technical choices: if our engineering projects are to be safe, for example, we need engineering professors who are skilled, not appointed in the name of social justice.

Selection problems. Another problem is that job applicants do not necessarily reflect the population. Few women apply to become army officers, and few men choose to work in social care. Employers face the problem that there may simply be insufficient candidates of the specified groups to fill their jobs – prompting standards to drop even more. And when well-qualified applicants from these groups are appointed, they may face scepticism about whether they were really chosen for their ability or simply to fill a quota.

Economic growth

World Bank data suggest that the best antidote to inequality is not redistribution, but a flourishing economy. The rich industrialised countries of North America, Europe and Oceania, with roughly three times the world average per capita GDP, are the most equal on the standard Gini measures. They are more equal than the generally poorer countries of South Asia, East Asia, the Middle East and North Africa. And they are far more equal than sub-Saharan Africa, with a per capita GDP of around a fifth of the world average. (Latin America, though only about 20 per cent below world average per capita GDP, is much less equal than any, but some of that may be due to regional peculiarities such as the large historic inequalities between the populations of European and local origin.)

A prosperous economy expands the opportunities available to the poorest more than most. The rich in a rich economy might become able to afford bigger superyachts, but the poor become able to afford better housing, transport, communications, food and clothing, and enjoy less onerous work and greater leisure.

Insofar as the prospect of earning high incomes in a dynamic economy incentivises people to invest, innovate and produce more, the whole community benefits through access to cheaper, better and more plentiful products. But if redistribution depresses economic activity, the community is left worse off – including the poorest, who may end up even worse off than they are today.

We cannot precisely measure how income equalisation affects economic growth, nor how far economic growth promotes equality. Certainly, a free society is likely to be an economically unequal one. But free societies also tend to be prosperous and democratic societies, which can

– and do – afford welfare measures to support the poorest, often raising them well above the average incomes of poor societies. For example, the average income of the *bottom fifth* of the US population, which the Congressional Budget Office puts at $22,500 a year even before the 68 per cent uplift they get from government transfer benefits, is six times higher than the average income of *everyone* in (socialist) Algeria and over thirty-five times the average in (communist) Cuba. As the American philosopher Harry Frankfurt (2015) notes, making everyone equally poor 'has very little to be said for it ... to eliminate income inequality cannot be, as such, our most fundamental goal.'

But thanks to recent decades of liberalisation and trade, the world is getting richer, and so the worst poverty is getting rarer. And is not our main objective in all this discussion about equality to make the poorest better off? From the point of view of morality, says Frankfurt (2015), 'it is not important that everyone should have *the same*. What is morally important is that each should have *enough*.'

14 DEMOCRACY AND EQUALITY

Public policies must have more than good intentions: they must deliver good results. But redistributive policies often do the opposite. Most of the spending does not go to the poorest, state services do not reflect diverse needs, and the larger the redistribution programme, the more life becomes politicised.

Coalition politics

Those who favour redistribution are confident that democracy can work in favour of poorer people: being greater in number than the rich, they have, if they choose to exercise it, the political weight to deliver redistribution.

But this is mere presumption: quite other coalitions of interest might raise the electoral majority they need to dictate events. For example, higher earners might form an alliance with the very poorest, agreeing to pay enough in tax transfers to eliminate their poverty – and in the process leave themselves better off than they are under today's system, which directs so much public spending to middle-class beneficiaries.

But the coalition that ultimately prevails may be even less charitable. In fact, it is the middle-income and slightly better-off groups who dominate the electoral process, not the very poor. There are simply more of them. The spread of incomes is bell-shaped, with low numbers of earners at the top and the bottom, and large numbers in the middle. Even among the lowest-paid half of the population, this group will dominate.

Middle-class domination of politics. And the middle-income and slightly well-off groups do dominate the electoral process. They are more numerous, pay the bulk of the taxes, and not surprisingly they get most of it back again in universal state benefits such as (depending on the country) pensions, free education and subsidised housing, healthcare and transport, all designed around their needs.

These benefits and services might be sold to the public as ways of helping the poor, but the middle class benefit from them too (and often benefit most: for example, the children of better-off families are more likely to attend state universities than those of poor families). Voting to expand state benefits and services might make the middle class feel charitable – but at no real cost to themselves.

The poor would be much better off if government budgets were simply divided equally between them. Yet much government spending currently goes to better-off groups such as farmers, students, older people, artists and intellectuals. Along the way, a significant proportion of the budget goes to the interest groups who promote these programmes, the staff and administrators who work in them, and the officials who design and implement them. It all promotes the self-perpetuation of middle-class welfare, since these groups (most of them better-off) have a shared coherent interest in preserving the system. The poor are a much less cohesive interest group and therefore much less influential over policy.

Politics over poverty. Hence the persistence of poverty, despite the rise and expansion of the welfare state in liberal democracies. Outcomes rest more on the political pressures and coalitions of the time, than on any rational strategy to relieve poverty or promote equality. This is something that academics too often ignore, assuming that the political system is democratic and fair: in fact, it is largely driven by interest groups. Far from reducing inequality, the realities of political power – in particular the political dominance of the middle class – mean that the political system *creates* inequality.

Limits to redistribution

In practice, there are limits to how much redistribution is achievable from taxing higher earners. Billionaire wealth would keep most governments going for a matter of days, not years. Not that it could be captured anyway: most of billionaires' wealth is in their businesses or their shares in businesses; it could not be easily liquidated by governments, and the value of those businesses would plummet if they tried.

Also, high progressive tax rates prompt higher earners to hire expensive advisers to shelter their money from confiscation. Wealthy people move their wealth, and indeed themselves, to lower-tax jurisdictions rather than lose it to high taxes. The more easily people can migrate or move their money, the less the tax that can be extracted from them. If wealthier people move out – as they did from the UK in the 1970s when the top rate of income tax was 83 per cent, with a 15 per cent surcharge on income from investments – that might make things *look* more equal, but the loss of human, physical and financial capital is a disaster for the country.

This point again encourages political deception and unequal treatment: politicians may set impressively high tax rates on high earners, but the burden is made bearable by various deductions and exemptions. That, in turn, creates public resentment at the unfairness that results. A lower rate for everyone, with few or no loopholes (the 'flat tax' concept), might raise more revenue with less avoidance, evasion and complaint.

How fair is forced redistribution? Just how fair is it to 'squeeze the rich' anyway, when most have earned their income fairly, paid tax on it, and made shrewd decisions on how to invest it?

Certainly, there are people who inherit wealth, and others who make money through their cronyism with politicians, using the political system to stifle competition, or getting political friends to steer government contracts their way. But it is the expansion of government that increases the opportunities for such cronyism: if there are monopolies, bailouts, subsidies, loans and contracts to be had, it is no surprise that some people will pursue them however they can. Cronyism is another example of inequality that is *created* by the political system.

The financial industry. The financial industry is often portrayed as an opportunity for the rich to get obscenely richer, and campaigners have linked the expansion of the finance sector in recent years to the rise in inequalities. But the financial industry is a highly productive one, adding to world productivity. All businesses need finance for their operations and trade, loans for investments, insurance, currency exchange, risk hedging, and much more. As greater international trade has expanded the size of many companies and diversified the places and the markets they operate in, such financial services have become even more important. Providing them requires skill, judgement and prudence in the face of risk.

Governments should be facilitating all this by keeping competition lively – though in practice, favourable tax treatments and 'too big to fail' policies and bailouts serve only to shore up incumbents and reduce that competition.

Political failure of the wealthy. It is a common conception that 'the rich' use their financial power to exploit and twist the political decision-making process in their favour. But lots of other interest groups and coalitions of interest groups are far more successful at that. The interests of 'the rich' – at least, those who have become rich through successful business enterprise rather than through political cronyism – would be *less* government and *lower* taxes, but the historical record does not indicate that this is how things are going. The equality narrative suggests that 'the rich' secured their own benefit by promoting politicians, such as Ronald Reagan and Margaret Thatcher, who supported the ideas of a 'smaller state'. But the smaller state never materialised. Governments have continued to expand, while taxes have risen, with top earners paying a disproportionate share.

Certainly, some people complain that the rich profit because they can take their income as capital gains, which are commonly taxed at lower rates than incomes. But relatively few people can do this, and capital gains are taxed at lower rates precisely because the investments behind them have been made out of income that was already taxed. Taking that into consideration, the real rate of capital gains taxes is generally far higher than income tax rates.

No political coherence. Talk of 'the rich' portrays them as a homogeneous economic class with similar interests. In fact, they are diverse individuals with diverse sources of income and wealth, from different business or professions, or from their particular talents in sport, culture or the arts. They have different values, motives, commitments, obligations and even political affiliations. They are far less of a coherent political force than the middle classes, who have been able to shape government programmes to their own benefit. Sadly, we cannot rely on politics to reduce inequality when politics is responsible for so much of it.

Who will equalise the equalisers?

Advocates of greater equality generally believe that it must be imposed by law: philanthropy alone is not enough. But then, rather than focusing on how to expand *voluntary* measures that might enhance equality, talent and energy is instead focused on using political authority to achieve it. For liberals, that is unsettling, because politics is about power, and power can be a dangerous thing.

The task may look modest enough – a few extra legislative measures such as wage regulations and wealth taxes, rather than any revolutionary replacement of the mixed-economy system. Nevertheless, power is needed to create and enforce those measures, and discretion is needed to determine which apply, at what level, to whom. *Somebody* has to take and enforce those decisions, so in the drive to make people equal in terms of their incomes, we find ourselves making an elite few *unequal* in terms of their political power.

That is a concern. Political elites have powers that not even the richest individuals can lay claim to – such as the power to make laws and to fine and imprison people if they do not comply with them. The key problem in political decision-making is not how to choose our politicians and administrators, but how to restrain them. The political process is a notoriously messy and irrational way to decide things. And it is particularly easy for authorities to abuse power – even unwittingly – in a task as simple as taking money off some people and giving it to others.

15 BARRIERS TO EQUALITY

If we want to use the power of the state to reduce inequality, we should first focus on the institutions that preserve equality and the barriers against it that governments themselves sometimes create.

Legal and civil equality

The first step in creating a just society is equality before the law. That does not mean treating all offenders similarly but treating similar cases in the same way. It does not mean only that people are subject to the same laws, because the laws may be unjust. Rather, it means the same impartial laws administered equally and justly – with equal access, judicial impartiality and the due process of law. There may be some exceptions – for example, the law may grant the police powers to use force to apprehend suspects; but such exceptions need substantial, relevant, rational and reasonable justification.

The same applies to civil or political equality. Civil equality implies an equal right to vote and to stand for office. But beyond that, a just political system also presumes free speech and the right to participate in debate, plus restraints on tactics such as political domination of the media, false arrest of opposition candidates, banning political parties, or intimidating candidates. The bigger that the state apparatus and state power is, the more these restraints are needed.

Equality and mobility

Advocates of greater equality argue that social mobility has declined. They see this as a symptom of inequality and demand government action to reverse it.

Statistical problems. Mobility is the ability to move by merit from one position to another – and is usually taken to mean how easily people can rise from less advantaged beginnings to a more advantaged position later, without irrelevant discriminatory barriers preventing them. The mobility statistics, however, do not measure the *ability* to rise without hindrance, only how many *do* rise, hindrances or no. Mobility statistics may be the best proxy we have for equality of opportunity, but mobility and opportunity are not the same things. The statistics lump in those who rise because they have ambition, a work ethic and determination with those who *could* rise but lack all those necessary motivations. As such they underestimate the prevalence of mobility among those who seek it.

Mobility and inequality. Despite this, the statistics do not suggest that inequality depresses mobility. Inequality was very high in the late nineteenth century and early twentieth century, and yet these were times of enormous mobility, exemplified by the rags-to-riches stories of Andrew Carnegie and Henry Ford. Rather, the key factor was more open competition and trade. In fast-growing economies, mobility is high, as ambitious people grasp the opportunities.

Mobility also rises because, if employers are to catch the rising economic tide, they cannot afford to maintain the traditional barriers against mobility. The rapid expansion of the IT industry in Hyderabad after India's 1990s reforms, for example, saw members of the lowest social castes rising into well-paid jobs because the booming industry valued their brains and abilities over their social class.

The statistics suggest that, despite rising inequality, mobility has not declined since the 1970s. The US is criticised for being unequal – and yet it is highly mobile. Is it such a bad thing if an unequal country is open to the success of any talented person?

Barriers against mobility

Though many see governments as the force needed to improve mobility, the reality is that state services, taxes, regulations and controls too often get in the way of it. Minimum wage laws are a barrier to getting a starter job and rising up the income ladder. Occupational licensing closes off professions to those who cannot afford long periods in expensive training. Regulations, often promoted in the name of public safety, can enable established businesses to keep out troublesome newcomers. Planning legislation pushes up housing costs, holding back young people.

Regressive taxes, consumption taxes and user charges fall most severely on the poor.

Innovators too are held back by government interventions. Anti-monopoly legislation holds back the expansion of the most successful companies and halts the build-up of productive capital. State monopolies in college education crowd out diverse and innovative kinds of learning and research. Bureaucracy depresses progress by channelling the productive effort of small and innovative companies into form-filling and box-ticking.

Redistributive taxes and benefits, meanwhile, strip productive wealth from some individuals while trapping others in relative poverty. Most poverty is because people are not working; but the design of social benefits often makes it difficult for them to get into work. If we are looking to remove barriers to economic mobility, we should certainly look at glass ceilings and other discrimination; but we should also remember the barriers raised by government action itself.

16 THE ROLE OF INEQUALITY

Do people want equality?

Is the general public really concerned about equality of outcome, and do they want to achieve it? On balance, it seems not. In opinion polls they routinely rank other things such as healthcare, prosperity, security, peace and safety above equality. Nor do they readily volunteer for higher taxes to promote it.

There is little indication that the public share the academics' ideal of an equal, uniform, uncompetitive society. Rather, they seem to prefer a diverse society in which they can aspire to rise up. The enormous demand for gambling perhaps attests to that – nearly every country in the world has a state lottery. Psychologists Christina Starmans, Mark Sheskin and Paul Bloom (2017) found that people prefer an unequal spread of incomes, as long as they sense that it is fair – with money going to hard workers, those with talent, and even the lucky lottery winners.

People are not even sure how equal or unequal their society is: when experimenters Oliver Hauser and Michael Norton (2017) asked subjects to pick their own society from a series of possible representations – showing, for example, a few rich people at the top and a large number at the bottom, or lots of rich people and few poor ones, or a large middle class and few at the top and the bottom – in general they could not, in some cases getting it completely wrong. (In general, they tended to underestimate the measured inequality in their society, causing equality-minded academics to lament their ignorance. But since, as we have seen, those measures ignore or underestimate a wide range of equalising factors, perhaps the public understand the true situation relatively well. Hence their lack of concern about it.)

Equal and unequal societies

Advocates of equality take it as so obviously beneficial that the burden of proof should fall on anyone who questions it. But this is not obvious. All real-world societies have inequalities, with hierarchies of wealth, income, power and social status in which people are treated differently. Even socialist societies still have inheritance, scholarships, honours, awards and even dachas for favoured artists. The unusual thing, if it ever existed (or survived beyond the first revolutionary ambitions) would be an equal society. The burden of proof sits more obviously on those who advocate such an innovation.

The functionality of inequality. There may well be good reasons why societies tend to be, and remain, unequal in so many ways – and, indeed, revert to inequality soon after their first experiments in equalisation. Inequalities and distinctions seem to reflect something fundamental in society. Unequal societies work: they have been around for millennia, they are still around, and are found everywhere. That is a more convincing record than the short-lived equalisation experiments of say, the Soviet Union, or Mao's China, or Pol Pot's Kampuchea or countless other socialist states in Asia, Africa and Latin America.

The question is *why* unequal societies work. It might be that inequality motivates people to train, get skills and improve their productivity, or that the prospect of entre-preneurial reward encourages risk-taking and innovation – all these things in turn boosting progress and prosperity. Or perhaps there is something more profound: possibly, as Edmund Burke thought, there is a 'wisdom' in the rules, customs and hierarchies that have been built up and lasted through the centuries.

Wealth and status

Wealth itself might have a useful social role, and not just as a way of building up productive capital. For example, F. A. Hayek (1976) notes that wealthy people can back their beliefs even when there is no prospect of material return, such as in the sponsorship of arts, education or research, and the promotion of new ideas. They can even support campaigns against oppressive governments who threaten the public with unjust laws.

The wealthy also have a social role as product pioneers. Usually, when an innovative product first appears, only wealthier people can afford it. They might even buy such products precisely to parade their wealth. But before long, everyone benefits – because these product pioneers quickly discover what is right and wrong with the product and the high prices they pay enable the manufacturer to improve it and mass-manufacture it more cheaply for a wider market. If millions of people today can afford smartphones, widescreen televisions, refrigerators or air travel, it is because a few years ago a few wealthy individuals tried out these products and found them worth having.

The role of hierarchies. Social status too may have a valuable social role. Hierarchies, starting with the family itself, imply inequality, but they help secure our social bonds. Seniority, honours or membership of a respected profession can be a useful indicator of whom we should take seriously. In a world of billions of people buzzing with different claims, these distinctions help focus our limited powers of attention and analysis.

The metaphor of 'dividing up the pie' naturally makes us imagine that equal shares are the only just solution. But, even in this misleading metaphor, other allocations may be perfectly rational: who wants the pie most, for example, or who most needs the calories? The equal shares assumption presumes that social and economic life is a deliberate collective enterprise, though it is really only what emerges when we live alongside and interact with others. And since people contribute different value to other members of the society, in different amounts, and have different needs and wants, why should not merit, need or desire not be more rational and functional standards than equality?

Growing the pie

Again, the 'equal pie' metaphor ignores the very thing that is most important about the wealth-creating process – that it is *dynamic*. Each of us aims to grow our own wealth, not take it from others – only criminals do that. And in an open, competitive economy the only way to grow your own wealth is to provide others with goods or services that they value – boosting their wealth too. Even though different people end up with different amounts of the 'expanding pie' of increasing wealth, everyone ends up with more, including the poorest. And those who do have more can afford to support the very poorest through welfare provision, public services and charity.

Productivity to end poverty. Advocates of equalisation accept that the poor did particularly well in the nineteenth and early twentieth centuries, a time of booming economies and incomes. Yet there were then no laws giving special treatment to trade unions, no minimum wage, relatively low taxation and public spending, and less of many other things that they suggest are important to equalisation. Rather, the rise in incomes was generated by inventions that raised productivity, bringing the world cheap clothing, manufactures, communication, transport, electricity, sanitation and much else. Soaring productivity allowed a progressive shortening of working hours and increase in leisure, while a wealthier society could afford higher standards in education, housing, welfare and other benefits for poorer citizens. All economic classes benefited and were far better off by the 1910s than they had been just 50 years earlier.

Improving standards. Despite world wars and other interruptions, this huge rise in living standards has continued. Life expectancy, education, literacy, safety, nutrition, disposable incomes and leisure time have all improved, while infant mortality, fatal accidents, famines and much else have fallen. And the ultimate source of all that is rising productivity – based on human ability, innovation, motivation, skill, human and physical capital, and hard work, all underpinned by liberal values and institutions, freedom of thought and action, property rights and free exchange.

All this has happened in a world of inequality, not despite it. Trying to extinguish inequality extinguishes the spark of enterprise and progress, as the otherwise similar North and South Korea, or the former East and West Germany, so startlingly demonstrate. In former socialist and supposedly equal countries such as Vietnam, the new rich are much richer than the poor, but even poorer workers are now buying televisions and motorbikes, and have every confidence that their prosperity will continue to rise. Inequality may be a driver of progress, or a consequence of it, or some combination of the two. But it seems certain that inequalities and diversity have profound social and economic importance; and we need greater thought about the potential consequences before choosing to suppress them.

17 CONCLUSION

Equality, then, is a much more troublesome concept than it first appears. It can mean so many different things that it is hard to know how to define it. People are unequal in many ways: they have different natural abilities, but they also make different choices, take different risks, and have different degrees of luck, all of which are factors in their economic success. These and much else make it very unclear how, or even if, we should do something about it.

Flawed measurement. We cannot even measure inequality well, given the sketchiness of the data and the fact that equalising taxes, social benefits and in-kind state benefits are ignored – and that the figures compare people at different stages in their lives. Once these factors are included, the prevalence of inequality falls dramatically. Comparing very different countries is even more problematic.

Flawed justifications. The common justifications for wanting greater equality are not convincing. The appeal to our universal humanity might justify the relief of poverty, but that is quite different from equality. Supposedly rational arguments, for example that faced with a blind choice we would all wish to live in an equal society, do not stack up when we reflect that different people have different attitudes to risk and the prospect of self-advancement. The idea that the rich simply get richer is not borne out by the facts, since fortunes rise and fall. And the alleged correlation of inequality with a range of social problems is weak and highly sensitive to what you include.

Flawed policies. Equalisation policies are not straightforward either. Equal pay sounds plausible until you reflect that different working hours and different family sizes will still produce accusations of unfairness and leave people unequally well off. Nor does it account for the fact that some jobs are simply more pleasant than others.

Given the impossibility of producing equal outcomes in the face of the vast array of different abilities, attitudes, actions and values of different people, the argument turns to the idea of equalising opportunities. But different families inevitably give their children a different start in life that affects their progress, though it is impossible to measure how much their success is due to that, or to hard work and motivation, or luck.

Contradictions. Redistribution is contradictory: it means treating people unequally in order to produce what *someone* believes is equality – though that judgement is inevitably subjective. And there is considerable danger in entrusting any politician or official with the power and discretion needed to force that judgement into reality.

Indeed, government often seems like the problem, steering resources to the middle classes, rather than the poor.

Collectivist mentality. The equality agenda is essentially collectivist, seeing individuals as subservient to this questionable social outcome. But most societies are unequal and the practical attempts to equalise them have been short-lived failures. We should consider the possibility that inequalities of wealth, status or hierarchy, and simple human diversity, might have important social functions, such as incentivising innovation, investment, productivity and enterprise. And we should remind ourselves that wealth is not something taken from others – except by criminals and governments – but something that is *created* in the everyday economic transactions between diverse individuals.

A better focus. We would do better to focus, not on equality, but on improving the condition of the poorest and dealing with the real social problems such as failing state schools, economic mismanagement and political power. Trying to end social problems by abolishing inequality is like trying to end crime by abolishing law. We need to address our social problems directly, rather than hoping that equality will correct them. Fixing failing schools, for example, would do more to boost mobility and equality than any amount of post-fact redistribution.

Focusing on equality and 'shares of the pie' ignores the dynamism of a free economy. Rising productivity and economic growth has produced huge advances in living standards for all. In the developed countries today, the poor live better, with more everyday conveniences, than yesterday's aristocrats could dream of. In 1836, Nathan Mayer Rothschild, the second richest man of all time, died of a tooth abscess: today we cure tooth abscesses with antibiotics; we even give antibiotics to animals.

The moral imperative. If you could push a button that would make the world's poorest twice as rich – but as a result make the world's richest three times as rich – would you not push it? Not that this is the real choice, since the most economically advanced economies are more equal, and in more ways, than poorer ones. But focus on inequality and we lose sight of what is truly important: not that everyone should be equal, but that everyone should have access to a decent standard of living.

REFERENCES

Booth, P. and Southwood, B. (2017) Poor thinking from Oxfam. *Economic Affairs* 9: 30–32.

Bowman, S. (2016) Seven reasons not to care about executive pay. *Medium*, 5 January 2016 (https://tinyurl.com/4bxeje7x).

Congressional Budget Office (2021) *The Distribution of Household Income, 2018.* August.

Frankfurt, H. G. (2015) *On Inequality.* Princeton University Press.

Galbraith, J. K. (1958) *The Affluent Society.* Boston MA: Houghton Mifflin.

Hasell, J. and Roser, M. (2019) How do we know the history of extreme poverty? (https://ourworldindata.org/extreme-history-methods). Our World In Data.

Hauser, O. P. and Norton, M. I. (2017) (Mis)perceptions of inequality. *Current Opinion in Psychology* 18: 21–25. (The authors' polling suggests that people's perceptions of their society do not accurately reflect measured equality and inequality.)

Hayek, F. A. (1976) *The Mirage of Social Justice.* University of Chicago Press. (Hayek argues that 'social justice' is not compatible with genuine justice and is such a vague and contentious term that it can never be a sound basis for public policy.)

International Monetary Fund (2018) Shadow economies around the world: what did we learn over the last 20 years? Working Paper WP 18/17.

International Monetary Fund (2020) *World Economic Outlook* (April), ch. 4.

Jacobs, L., Llanes, E., Moore, K., Thompson, J. and Volz, A. H. (2021) Wealth concentration in the United States using an expanded measure of net worth. Research Department Working Paper 21-6. Federal Reserve Bank of Boston.

Kelley, J. and Evans, M. D. R. (2017) Societal income inequality and individual subjective well-being: results from 68 societies and over 200,000 individuals, 1981–2008. *Social Science Research* 62(1): 1–23. (The authors' very extensive polling across the world suggests that in developing nations inequality is not harmful but probably beneficial to people's well-being.)

Milanovic, B. L., Van Der Weide, R., Milanovic, B. L. and Van Der Weide, R. (2014) Inequality is bad for growth of the poor (but not for that of the rich). Policy Research Working Paper Series 6963, The World Bank.

Morgan, M. and Neef, T. (2020) What's new about income inequality in Europe (1980–2019)? Issue Brief 20/24, World Inequality Lab.

National Bureau of Economic Research (2017) The gender pay gap widens with age. *The Digest*, no. 7.

Norberg, J. (2016) *Progress: Ten Reasons to Look Forward to the Future*. London: Oneworld Publications.

Office for National Statistics (2021) *Effects of Taxes and Benefits on UK Household Income: Financial Year Ending 2020.*

Pew Research Center (2013) What men, women value in a job. In *On Pay Gap, Millennial Women Near Parity – For Now* (https://tinyurl.com/2p8w2cz9).

Ramsey Solutions (2021) How many millionaires actually inherited their wealth? (https://tinyurl.com/2p8wfu7t).

Ravallion, M. (2016) Are the world's poorest being left behind? *Journal of Economic Growth* 21, 139–164 (https://doi.org/10.10 07/s10887-016-9126-7).

Rawls, J. (1971) *A Theory of Justice.* Cambridge, MA: Harvard University Press.

Roser, M. and Ortiz-Ospina, E. (2013) Global extreme poverty (https://ourworldindata.org/extreme-poverty). Our World In Data.

Starmans, C., Sheskin, M. and Bloom, P. (2017) Why people prefer unequal societies. *Nature Human Behaviour* 1, Article 0082. (The authors' polling shows that when asked about the ideal distribution of wealth in their country, people prefer unequal societies as long as they are fair.)

World Bank (2016) *Poverty and Shared Prosperity 2016: Taking on Inequality* (https://doi.org/10.1596/978-1-4648-0958-3).

World Bank (2019) PovcalNet (http://iresearch.worldbank.org/PovcalNet/data.aspx).

World Population Review. Wealth inequality by country 2022 (https://tinyurl.com/2p9xkbww).

Worstall, T. (2019) Oxfam's inequality claims aren't just misleading. They're untrue. *CapX*, 21 January (https://capx.co/oxfams-inequality-claims-arent-just-misleading-theyre-untrue/).

Further reading

The equality narrative

Pickett, K. and Wilkinson, R. (2010) *The Spirit Level: Why Equality Is Better for Everyone.* London: Penguin. (Suggests that almost every social problem, from mental illness through violence to illiteracy, is a product of how unequal a society is, not how rich it is.)

Piketty, T. (2017) *Capital in the Twenty-First Century.* Cambridge, MA: Harvard University Press. (Suggests that the return on capital is always greater than economic growth in general, meaning that the rich inevitably get richer.)

Stiglitz, J. (2013) *The Price of Inequality.* London: Penguin. (Criticises market instability and political failure and argues that the results are fundamentally unfair.)

Rebuttals of the narrative

Arnott, R., Bernstein, W. and Wu, L. (2015) The myth of dynastic wealth: the rich get poorer. *Cato Journal* 35(3). (Demonstrates the flaws in Piketty's contention that the rich get richer and shows how and why wealth dissipates.)

Delsol, J-P., Lecaussin, N. and Martin, E. (eds) (2017) *Anti-Piketty: Capital for the 21st Century.* Washington, DC: Cato Institute Press. (Twenty economists, historians and tax experts examine inequality, growth, wealth and capital, critiquing Thomas Piketty's analysis and solutions.)

Snowdon, C. (2010) *The Spirit Level Delusion: Fact-Checking the Left's New Theory of Everything.* London: Democracy Institute. (Argues that the *Spirit Level* contention lacks empirical evidence and falsely attributes social problems to inequality rather than wider causes.)

General critiques

Bourne, R. and Edward, C. (2019) *Exploring Wealth Inequality.* Washington, DC: Cato Institute Press. (Argues that wealth inequality has increased modestly, but mainly because of economic progress that has been highly beneficial to the broader public.)

Bourne, R. and Snowdon, C. (2016) Never mind the gap: why we shouldn't worry about inequality. IEA Discussion Paper 70. London: Institute of Economic Affairs. (Critiques the ideas that the distribution of income and wealth is a zero-sum game and can be easily controlled, which take our focus off the goal of improving the living standards of the poorest.)

Cavenagh, M. (2002) *Against Equality of Opportunity.* Oxford: Clarendon Press. (Argues that equality of opportunity is such a vague and catch-all phrase that it is useless as a guide to policy.)

Conrad, E. (2016) *The Upside of Inequality: How Good Intentions Undermine the Middle Class.* New York: Portfolio. (Argues that the obsession with inequality is misguided, dulls incentives, and creates a shortage of the trained talent we need for today's knowledge-led economy.)

Letwin, W. (ed.) (1983) *Against Equality: Readings on Economic and Social Policy.* London: Palgrave. (Series of essays by prominent philosophers, economists and social scientists, questioning the orthodox narrative of inequality and redistribution.)

Sowell, T. (2016) *Wealth, Poverty, and Politics.* New York: Basic Books. (Explores the reasons for income and wealth disparities between and among nations. It examines the effect of different combinations of different geographic, cultural, political and other factors on economic growth.)

Sowell, T. (2018) *Discrimination and Disparities.* New York: Basic Books (revised and enlarged edition, 2019). (Challenges single-factor explanations of economic differences such as discrimination or exploitation, and explains why some of the policies built on them have proved so counterproductive.)

Watkins, D. and Brook, Y. (2016) *Equal Is Unfair: America's Misguided Fight against Income Inequalities.* New York: St. Martin's Press. (Critiques the inequality narrative and redistribution policies such as CEO wage caps and minimum wages, and argues that the narrative damages economic mobility.)

Debates

Furchtgott-Roth, D. (ed.) (2020) *United States Income, Wealth, Consumption, and Inequality.* Oxford University Press. (Essays exploring US income inequality, arguing that it is not easily quantified, leading to different explanations and policy responses.)

Narveson, J. and Sterba, J. P. (2010) *Are Liberty and Equality Compatible? (For and Against).* Cambridge University Press. (Two philosophers debate whether the political principle of 'negative' liberty is compatible with equality.)

ABOUT THE IEA

The Institute is a research and educational charity (No. CC 235 351), limited by guarantee. Its mission is to improve understanding of the fundamental institutions of a free society by analysing and expounding the role of markets in solving economic and social problems.

The IEA achieves its mission by:

- a high-quality publishing programme
- conferences, seminars, lectures and other events
- outreach to school and college students
- brokering media introductions and appearances

The IEA, which was established in 1955 by the late Sir Antony Fisher, is an educational charity, not a political organisation. It is independent of any political party or group and does not carry on activities intended to affect support for any political party or candidate in any election or referendum, or at any other time. It is financed by sales of publications, conference fees and voluntary donations.

In addition to its main series of publications, the IEA also publishes (jointly with the University of Buckingham), *Economic Affairs*.

The IEA is aided in its work by a distinguished international Academic Advisory Council and an eminent panel of Honorary Fellows. Together with other academics, they review prospective IEA publications, their comments being passed on anonymously to authors. All IEA papers are therefore subject to the same rigorous independent refereeing process as used by leading academic journals.

IEA publications enjoy widespread classroom use and course adoptions in schools and universities. They are also sold throughout the world and often translated/reprinted.

Since 1974 the IEA has helped to create a worldwide network of 100 similar institutions in over 70 countries. They are all independent but share the IEA's mission.

Views expressed in the IEA's publications are those of the authors, not those of the Institute (which has no corporate view), its Managing Trustees, Academic Advisory Council members or senior staff.

Members of the Institute's Academic Advisory Council, Honorary Fellows, Trustees and Staff are listed on the following page.

The Institute gratefully acknowledges financial support for its publications programme and other work from a generous benefaction by the late Professor Ronald Coase.

Other books recently published by the IEA include:

Education, War and Peace: The Surprising Success of Private Schools in War-Torn Countries
James Tooley and David Longfield
ISBN 978-0-255-36746-2; £10.00

Killjoys: A Critique of Paternalism
Christopher Snowdon
ISBN 978-0-255-36749-3; £12.50

Financial Stability without Central Banks
George Selgin, Kevin Dowd and Mathieu Bédard
ISBN 978-0-255-36752-3; £10.00

Against the Grain: Insights from an Economic Contrarian
Paul Ormerod
ISBN 978-0-255-36755-4; £15.00

Ayn Rand: An Introduction
Eamonn Butler
ISBN 978-0-255-36764-6; £12.50

Capitalism: An Introduction
Eamonn Butler
ISBN 978-0-255-36758-5; £12.50

Opting Out: Conscience and Cooperation in a Pluralistic Society
David S. Oderberg
ISBN 978-0-255-36761-5; £12.50

Getting the Measure of Money: A Critical Assessment of UK Monetary Indicators
Anthony J. Evans
ISBN 978-0-255-36767-7; £12.50

Socialism: The Failed Idea That Never Dies
Kristian Niemietz
ISBN 978-0-255-36770-7; £17.50

Top Dogs and Fat Cats: The Debate on High Pay
Edited by J. R. Shackleton
ISBN 978-0-255-36773-8; £15.00

School Choice around the World … And the Lessons We Can Learn
Edited by Pauline Dixon and Steve Humble
ISBN 978-0-255-36779-0; £15.00

Other IEA publications

Comprehensive information on other publications and the wider work of the IEA can be found at www.iea.org.uk. To order any publication please see below.

Personal customers

Orders from personal customers should be directed to the IEA:

IEA
2 Lord North Street
FREEPOST LON10168
London SW1P 3YZ
Tel: 020 7799 8911, Fax: 020 7799 2137
Email: sales@iea.org.uk

Trade customers

All orders from the book trade should be directed to the IEA's distributor:

NBN International (IEA Orders)
Orders Dept.
NBN International
10 Thornbury Road
Plymouth PL6 7PP
Tel: 01752 202301, Fax: 01752 202333
Email: orders@nbninternational.com

IEA subscriptions

The IEA also offers a subscription service to its publications. For a single annual payment (currently £42.00 in the UK), subscribers receive every monograph the IEA publishes. For more information please contact:

Subscriptions
IEA
2 Lord North Street
FREEPOST LON10168
London SW1P 3YZ
Tel: 020 7799 8911, Fax: 020 7799 2137
Email: accounts@iea.org.uk